Break Free with Goddess

Wiccans—How You Can Get Free of Worry, Illness and Anxiety and Enjoy Abundance, Health and Confidence

from GoddessHasYourBack.com

Moonwater SilverClaw

Wiccan High Priestess
Blogger/Founder of
GoddessHasYourBack.com
with visitors from 191 countries

A QuickBreakthrough Publishing Edition

Copyright © 2018 Johanna Ellen Mac Leod
ISBN: 0998427322
ISBN-13: 978-0998427324

All rights reserved. No part of this book may be reproduced or transmitted in any form by any means electronic or mechanical, including photocopying, recording or by any information storage and retrieval system without written permission from the publisher.

More copies are available from the publisher with the imprint QuickBreakthrough Publishing. For more information about this book contact: askawitchnow@gmail.com

This book was developed and written with care. Names and details were modified to respect privacy.

Disclaimer: The author and publisher acknowledge that each person's situation is unique, and that readers have full responsibility to seek consultations with health, financial, spiritual and legal professionals. The author and publisher make no representations or warranties of any kind, and the author and publisher shall not be liable for any special, consequential or exemplary damages resulting, in whole or in part, from the reader's use of, or reliance upon, this material.:

Other Books by Moonwater SilverClaw:
- Goddess Has Your Back
- Goddess Style Weight Loss
- Goddess Walks Beside You
- The Hidden Children of the Goddess
- Be a Wiccan Badass
- Beyond the Law of Attraction to Real Magick
- Goddess Reveals Your Enchanted Light

Praise for Moonwater SilverClaw:

• "Moonwater was telling me about her **weight loss program** and it sounded like something I could do that didn't cost me more than the normal groceries I buy, anyway. I started with an egg omelet in the morning with mushrooms and spinach. ... In two weeks, I lost 7 lbs. I had a couple of days of eating what I wanted but not overeating. Then right back to *Goddess Style*. I feel great and eat what the Goddess gives us." – Denise Kopplinger

• "In her book *The Hidden Children of the Goddess*, Moonwater brings Wicca to life, enveloping you in the mystery and magick of the Craft. Her writing talent is amazing! Her kindness and even sense of fun is ever present throughout her writing. Moonwater expresses profound Wicca concepts through examples in her own life experience. Wicca actually saved her life. and empowered her to leave an abusive marriage, and this shows the power of this sacred path to positively change the course of our lives, too. Moonwater's stories personally inspire me, and I am confident that they will inspire you also." – Rev. Patrick McCollum, internationally recognized spiritual leader working for human rights, social justice, and equality; the 2010 recipient of the Mahatma Gandhi Award for the Advancement of Pluralism.

• "Religion scholars in the future will likely view Moonwater SilverClaw as the pivotal voice that helped change the discourse on Wicca. In her book **Goddess Has Your Back,** Moonwater reveals Wicca as a very positive and ultimately uplifting spirituality choice. She demystifies the religion's taboos and spooky stereotypes through her unintimidating presentation that clarifies the topic. She introduces the Goddess and the magick rituals that, when used properly, can positively impact your everyday life. The author relays her very personal perspective on the subject and shows how to integrate the philosophies and practices of the centuries-old religion. Looking for a fresh perspective on spiritual growth? Read what Moonwater SilverClaw has to say." – Stacy D. Horn

• "Moonwater's writing will give you a portrait of a woman who lives her faith, and whose life was saved by it. Because so many lives, my own included, were irrevocably changed by Wicca, were given new focus, new purpose, and perhaps most importantly, new personal power to realize one's dreams and ambitions.... It's a story about making your own happy endings, about rescuing yourself...." – Jason Pitzl-Waters, former blogger at WildHunt.org

Visit Moonwater's blog: www.GoddessHasYourBack.com

Moonwater SilverClaw

CONTENTS*

These are highlights. There is much more material in this book!

Dedication and Acknowledgments	6
Break Free with Goddess	7
Section One: Freedom from Worry	8
Section Two: Freedom to Express Yourself	27
Section Three: Freedom to Be Healthy	49
Section Four: Freedom for Abundance	77
Section Five: Freedom to Be Creative	89
Section Six: Freedom to Be Me	105
Section Seven: Protect Yourself	137
Bonus Material	159
About the Author; Special Offer to Reader of this Book	167,168
About Online Course *Goddess Style Weight Loss*	166
Excerpt from *Goddess Has Your Back*	168
Excerpt from *Beyond the Law of Attraction to Real Magick*	171

DEDICATION AND ACKNOWLEDGEMENTS

This book is dedicated to the God and Goddess. Thanks to Tom Marcoux for editing. Thanks to Kay Pannell for her guidance and friendship.

Thank you and blessings to you, the reader.

GoddessHasYourBack.com

For insights about spells, rituals, and more
**Visit GoddessHasYourBack.com
for blog posts and to sign up for
Moonwater SilverClaw's E-newsletter.**

Break Free with Goddess

Do you feel free? Imagine that Goddess can help you break free of anything binding you down and holding you back. That would be great, right?

Wicca is all about freedom. You get to choose which Deities with whom you have a relationship. You're free to choose what you believe, how you practice and how you live your life.

Make a Jailbreak with Goddess

Do you sometimes feel imprisoned by fear or something else? I'm with you about that. Over the years, I've faced times when I've felt so fearful. I worried a lot. It's Goddess who has helped me embrace my full potential. Truly. A dyslexic person who writes a blog and eight books? With Goddess's help and a team of editors that became possible for me.

What do *you* want to be possible for you?

Here are the Sections of this Book:
1. Freedom from Worry
2. Freedom to Express Yourself
3. Freedom to Be Healthy
4. Freedom for Abundance
5. Freedom to Be Creative
6. Freedom to Be Me
7. Protect Yourself

Bonus Material

This book is designed to help you discover your own new path. You'll begin to truly *free yourself* of binding elements and live with full joy and fulfillment.

Let's get started.

Section One:
Freedom from Worry

Ever worry about how you won't stop worrying? I know redundant, right?

Still, I've become tired of being sick and tired.

I was even mad at myself for being mad.

You get the picture.

Sometimes, I feel like I wish I could order my life at a restaurant with the Goddess as my server. I would order my life by saying to the Goddess, "This is *not* the life I was asking for. Didn't You hear? I was asking for the No-pain Special."

Can you relate to this?

Do you notice how everybody has become masters of complaining?

I realize that there is plenty to complain about. Sometimes, on Facebook, I really don't have the words to express my condolences when someone loses a friend or pet. I resort to the teary face emoticon.

Imagine, when you're worrying, and Goddess says, "I've got this. I'm holding it. I'm holding you. I'm taking care of it."

I'm not saying that Poof!—all worries just evaporate.

Then again, sometimes, they do for a few minutes.

The idea in this section is to pay attention to when you *do* get Divine help. We need to aim to get out of our own way.

You might hold this affirmation: "Goddess has it. Somehow, this can work out for my good and the good of all involved."

Every day, I see my husband do a process in which he taps his chest—taps his heart chakra—and says, "I am one hundred percent safe." He tells me that it helps. In that moment, he *is* safe. And in this way, he's paying attention.

How do you pay attention?

Perhaps, you'd find it helpful to create a new Habit of Thought. Tap your heart area and say, "Goddess has this."

I'll get specific. One time, I felt an avalanche of worry. Why? I needed a new car. Maybe not new. But new to me!

The obstacle. Money.

Isn't that often the problem?

I'd seen a second-best car. It wasn't "second best." It was really "yuck." In my price range. I did ***not*** like it.

The night before going to get the car. I did a meditation. "Lord and Lady, please help me with this car. I need low mileage, good mpg and low repair costs. I want a purple blue and something I can afford. Please make my way clear."

The next morning, I got an intuitive feeling. *Go to the*

Toyota lot.

The feeling wouldn't go away.

I took it as an intuitive "order"—or Goddess saying, 'I got this.'

My appointment to get the "yuck" car was about an hour away.

But I said to a family member, "Yeah, we'll go get that car. But just before we do that, *let's stop at the Toyota lot first.*"

We pulled up to the lot. My new brilliant blue car was right there! In front of all the other cars. I then found out that someone had bought the car new, driven it 9,000 miles and returned it. The dealership had to discount this preowned and current year vehicle. So, I could afford it. What they say is true—you drive a car off the lot and BOOM! It loses value.

So, I could get a car I loved, for a reasonable price.

Thank you, Goddess!

See, Goddess, in her way, said, "I got this."

How can we invite Goddess to help? What does She want? Perhaps, something as small as lighting a candle. Present a simple offering as a thank you to the Goddess.

Section One:
Freedom from Worry #1

The Wiccan Advantage When Dealing with Worry

The "I am so worried," Zoe said.

"Tell me more," I said.

"My whole household is down with the flu. Except me. Well, I'm starting to cough. I don't how much longer I can take the pressure," she said.

Saying "Don't worry" won't do Zoe any good at this moment.

When's the last time you have been seriously worried? Is it happening now?

I've noticed that worry gets more intense about things we really cannot control.

What can you do?

We, Wiccans, have an advantage: We can do an empowering ritual.

The "Let Go" Meditation/Ritual

What you will need:

- One white candle
- Banishing oil or extra virgin olive oil
- Banishing incense or your favorite scent
- Ritual tools
- Cakes and wine

This is a truly simple candle ritual you can do to get some relief from worry.

Cast the Circle in the usual manner. (For specifics about Casting a Circle, see my blog article at

http://bit.ly/2DuaMao)

Consecrate and charge your candle with your holy water and your incense. Dress your candle with your oil. (For specifics about dressing a candle, see my blog article at http://bit.ly/2DF8hFC)

Start belly-breathing (taking big breaths in and out—slowly) and light the candle.

Envision all your worry and fretting going into the candle's flame. That is, envision all your worry as a black smoke flowing out of your mouth with each breath out. The flame draws all the black smoke.

Say:

In this moment,
I let go.
Goddess take this from me.
God strengthen me.
So mote it be.

Continue your meditation on the candle, breathing out all your worries as the black smoke.

When you're done, thank the God and Goddess for Their support. Let the rest of the candle burn out.

Warning: Never leave a candle burning unattended.

Do the Cakes and Wine ceremony.

Close the Circle.

May this ritual bring you relief and peace.

Section One:
Freedom from Worry #2

Wiccans and Rising Up from Discouragement and Disappointment

The car roared through the intersection and barely missed me.

How? I was not in the intersection because a clear thought came to me: "Not yet." This meant, I was to avoid stepping on the accelerator and jumping my car forward when the light turned green.

You'd think that after a real experience of having my intuition, or Goddess's voice, protect me, I'd have a whole new perspective.

I might even hope for my life to continue to be blessed with such miraculous protection.

But I have had a problem with hope.

Why would someone ask someone for a date? For the hope that the person would say "yes" and a good relationship could begin.

Why would someone attend college? For the hope that the person would gain better employment.

Recently, I was talking with a friend about a Wiccan perspective of hope.

"I don't know if I'm the one to respond to that idea," I replied.

You see, I've lived much of my life—before this moment—by protecting myself from hope. By not hoping, disappointment cannot touch me. Or so I thought.

What I've learned is: Many of us are afraid of being let down. But by *not* hoping, **we let ourselves down before anything really begins.** We take away our own energy. We find ourselves in a space that is both familiar and painful. You might even say, we are almost comfortable in that familiar pain—comfortably numb.

How do you invite God and Goddess into this situation?

My Realization about Hope

In the recent few days, I realized something about my relationship with hope. I cannot logic my way to feeling hopeful. My logical mind can focus on all the times I've done something, and true blessings arose. I changed my life for the better with one particular email message that turned a romantic relationship into the love of my life. I met certain neighbors and joined my first coven. Recounting my blessings does not change my feelings. (Okay, having clinical depression is in the mix here.)

If logic won't get me to hope, what can? Moving. Ritual.

Here are five ways for Wiccans to shift to a hopeful approach to life:

1. Raise Energy

You can sing, chant, dance, use breath control and many

other techniques to raise energy. If you are in a tough spot, doing the above methods can help motivate and even change your outlook on many problems.

Using your strong emotions, you can focus energy to your Will.

When you raise energy, you can focus the related power to help create the outcome you desire.

2. Breathe in Light; Breathe out Pain

Here is a simple exercise that you can do to lessen the pain and stress of disappointment.

Say to yourself:

I breathe in the light of love from the Gods.

(Visualize the white light all around you. As you breathe in deeply, the white light enters your body, filling your lungs and nurturing your soul.)

I breathe out my pain and sadness.

(Visualize breathing out your pain as black smoke. It is neutralized safely by the Gods.)

With this exercise you can release the pain of worry and disappointment.

3. Shift Your Thoughts by Shifting Your Body

Ritualized movement can place you in a positive frame of mind. I enjoy the movement of drawing the pentacle in the air with my athame during ritual.

Additionally, the act of Casting the Circle helps me settle my mind and know that I am in the sacred space. This is why we cast Circle the same way each time. It is to help our subconscious mind settle down to the work at hand. This literally changes your mind to be in the presence of the

Gods.

4. Cultivate Your "Believing Eyes Friends"

Julia Cameron, author of *The Artist Way*, writes about how we need friends who have "believing eyes." These are friends who can believe for us—even when we cannot believe for ourselves at this moment.

We often get lost in our own beliefs. "Oh, I can't do that." Or "Oh, that will never happen." We literally cannot see a worldview outside of ourselves. Our vision is limited by self-condemning beliefs.

This is why it is important to nurture friendships with healthy people who hold our dreams in a loving way.

5. Light a Candle and Ask for Help from God and Goddess

Light a candle and ask the God and Goddess to intervene on your behalf. Say a prayer. Or do a ritual.

In summary, I've shared that hopeful thoughts and feelings—before this moment—have not been a primary part of my life.

Here's something strange. In writing this section, I am acting in a hopeful manner. My hope is that you'll find value in this above section.

Section One:
Freedom from Worry #3

A Spell to Keep You Safe When Traveling by Car

"I wasn't even driving at the time, and still I was in another car accident!" my friend, Lesley, said. "Moonwater, please give me some kind of protection. After being in three accidents, I'm afraid of driving now."

Lesley asked me to write up a simple ritual to enhance her protection when she is in a car. This would help her quiet down her fear.

Have you been in a car accident? When you get into a car do you have some fearful thoughts about getting into another accident? During a holiday season, many of us fear to encounter drunk drivers on the road.

Some time ago, when I was in a car accident while a friend was driving, I only had a mild case of whiplash. I was grateful to the God and Goddess for protecting me from anything more severe.

Today, I have a protection sigil in my car, and the sigil has saved me from a number of fender-benders.

How significant are the risks of driving? I looked at the MADD (Mothers Against Drunk Driving) website and found this: "About 4,000 drivers are killed each year with drugs in their systems. This doesn't count those who had drugs in their system without test results, or those killed by drivers with drugs in their system."

The MADD website continues with: "During weekday daytime, 12.1% of drivers tested positive for an illegal drug; 10.3% tested positive for prescription and OTC medications. During weekend nighttime, 15.2% of drivers tested positive for an illegal drug; 7.3% tested positive for prescription and OTC medications."

Perhaps, you join me in looking on these percentages with concern. How can we protect ourselves and our loved ones, especially during a holiday season? With the ritual below.

Ritual for Your Safety While Traveling by Car
What you will need:
- Protection While Driving Sigil
- Protection incense
- Ritual tools
- Altar

Preparation:

Create your sigil as seen above.

Use a virgin sheet of parchment or plain paper (which has not been written upon) and recreate the sigil image above.

Set up your altar.

Take your ritual bath.

Meditate on how you want to be protected by the Gods when you drive, and you want that your fear about driving diminishes.

Ritual:

Cast Circle in the usual manner.

Cleanse the sigil with your holy water.

Charge the sigil by holding it over the incense. As you do so, chant three times:

Protection surrounds me,
Fear releases me!
Where the rubber meets road,
Let no worry have its hold!

Take your charged sigil and go to the East and say:

I call upon the East to open the doors to the wisdom of protection for me!

Take your sigil to the South and say:

I call upon the South to stoke the flames of fearlessness within me.

Take your sigil to the West and say:

I call upon the West to wash serenity over me while I drive.

Take your sigil to the North and say:

I call upon the North to ground me in protection from others on the road.

Carry your sigil back to the East and say:

So Mote it Be!

Do the Cakes and Wine Ceremony.

Close your Circle.

Use this ritual to create a charged sigil for your protection. The sigil will also help you stay calm and strong while on the road.

May this sigil ritual keep you safe.

Section One:
Freedom from Worry #4

Loving the Goddess

Many years ago, I didn't have the God and Goddess in my life. And I was the worst for it. The day I first met the God and Goddess, I had just endured a tough time.

My then boyfriend (soon to be first husband) had said some truly rude things. It shook me up. This was someone I loved, and I had devoted so much energy and attention to him. And he mistreated me?! In a huff, he left the house.

I went to the back deck of the house. I was alone. My thoughts were swirling. Darkness, pain and a dash of hopelessness.

I closed my eyes for meditation. But I snapped them open. I was not settling down.

I closed my eyes again. Some moments passed. Then I felt a presence. The presence got more defined and soon I felt it was not just one presence but two!

I breathed in and out deeply. I focused on Their presence.

Only 17 years old, I had felt nervous several times. But this was different. I was unnerved! But as the God and Goddess seemed to get closer, my discomfort faded away. I was in the presence of the Gods!

I couldn't think of anything to say to Them. It didn't matter. I was flooded with the feeling—and the knowing—of peace and love.

If you feel lonely or lost, consider meditation. For many of us, meditation will simply give us some moments of calm and peace. And sometimes, we may actually experience, close up, the presence of the Gods.

Whether this happens to you once in one hundred sessions or more, one experience of total connection with the Gods will be the sustenance for a lifetime.

Section One:
Freedom from Worry #5

Prayer for Peace

Recently, I've seen horrible atrocities on the broadcast news. Certain people consider themselves superior simply because of their skin color. Broadcast news reveals that some people spew forth hatred that culminates in violence.

What can we do?

As Wiccans, we have the blessing of connecting directly to the God and Goddess.

Here is a short prayer for peace.

Prayer for Peace

Strong Lord and Gracious Lady,
Give us relief from the tempers that flare
Let hate fade and grace fill the air.
Let peace cool the fanned flames of hate,
Make unbridled anger abate.

Let us come together in peace
With kindness and grace.
So mote it be.

Section One:
Freedom from Worry #6

How You Can Get Access to the Deepest Wiccan Knowledge

"Why do I need a mentor?" Jessica asked. "So many books could help me learn what I need to, right?"

"Yes, you can learn a lot from books," I began. "But the good stuff, the advanced stuff, isn't in books. That's where a mentor comes in."

Having a mentor, you get to go deeper than any book can offer. Authors, if they're candid, will admit this.

So much to learn isn't available in books. You can only learn certain secrets and techniques from someone who has actual experience—which was supported by their own mentors.

Having a mentor helps you focus your efforts and keeps you safe from making rookie mistakes. Your mentor can help you get out of trouble, if you get in over your head.

Mentors guide you to do energy work correctly, so you

don't hurt yourself. Your mentor can help you control your energy in your spellwork.

Mentors often fill several roles: friend, teacher, confidant, priest/priestess and more.

Books describe how to do things. Mentors help you *experience* things. Big difference.

If you read about rollercoasters in a book, you wouldn't know the experience of riding a rollercoaster. Oh, the book could express, in lovely poetry, something about the feelings and the motion.

Only your actual ride on the rollercoaster brings true understanding.

The truth is: Your mentor is crucial for your real advancement. Mentors will have the right answers at the right time, when you need them.

If you're looking to deepen your knowledge of the Craft, it may be time to find a mentor. For more about mentors, visit GoddessHasYourBack.com for the article "How Wiccans Can Find Trustworthy Mentors – Avoid Plastic Shamans and Charlatans." You can use this link:

http://bit.ly/2ipJUBu

Section Two:
Freedom to Express Yourself

"I'm going to wear my pentacle pendant," I said.

My husband got that familiar, wincing look on his face.

I wanted to say, "Screw your college reunion and all of those intolerant, religious nuts." I didn't say that. I was saving it to write it here.

We kept talking. And talking. Over a couple of days.

(By the way, my husband doesn't subscribe to that college's religion. He was attending for making business contacts.)

Then, the idea arose in my mind. I'll just turn my pendant around. It has the green man of the other side. Not so scary for those religious nuts. It was a good idea. *Thank you, Goddess.*

Know that Goddess is watching over you. She's looking for ways for you to be true to yourself—*and* navigate this world.

You help Goddess by *not* giving up. Keep talking. Keep looking. Ask Goddess for Her guidance.

It's important that you find good, appropriate and safe ways to express yourself. Why? You'll feel free! You'll feel like you're being heard.

Still, the truth is: Some people do not want to—or they cannot—hear you. Move past them. Connect with your Wiccan and Pagan tribe.

Recently, Facebook hit me with the "real name" rule.

Moonwater SilverClaw *is* my real name. It's my pen name as well as my magical name. Every time I attend, PantheaCon, my name badge says "Moonwater SilverClaw."

But I can imagine Facebook whining "but it's not on your driver's license."

Well, Facebook, you can take that and …

I felt like the Facebook team was stifling my freedom to express myself. Finally, I just played along. Now, I must start some Facebook chats with "This is Moonwater …"

However, I am still expressing myself. That's what counts.

I heard a friend say, "Now is what counts."

"Yes," I said, "And it's even better when you find ways to express yourself."

Find ways to express yourself.

I *am* Moonwater SilverClaw here in this book and on my blog GoddessHasYourBack.com.

Section Two:
Freedom to Express Yourself #1

Wiccans and Standing Against Oppression and Sexual Harassment

"Wiccans are being oppressed. There's a reason why many of us stay in the broom closet," my friend Aaron said. "What about the people who denied Wiccans the right to place a pentacle on their tombstone?"

What can we do about oppression? Speak up!

As I write this, women have come forward to speak the truth about sexual harassment and to identify those who have abused them.

I celebrate women standing up and speaking out.

I also realize that many women and girls have been pushed by society to shut up and take abuse. Over the years, I have even found that I tended to shut up because I didn't want to "be a bitch." (It's hard to admit that I had fallen for society's lie about "who is a bitch.")

There Is a Horrible Myth about "Being a Bitch" When One Is Really Being Assertive

From the time I was a child through my teen years, I saw how assertive female individuals were harassed for standing up for themselves.

But it is worse. I've read about how people tend to internalize the authority figures' voices—in their own minds. If I spoke up, I would be called a bitch. I even said to friends, "I don't want to be a bitch."

My own husband says, "You're not doing that. Instead, you're being *assertive*. Assertive is *not* the same thing as aggressive."

Let's pay attention to this point: Using the "bitch" label is how many people try to keep women "in line." Enough of that!

Currently, I'm in the middle of a dispute with an online retailer. I just wanted my money back, and the online retailer denied my request. So, I went to the payment vendor and asked them to resolve it.

The payment vendor sided with the online retailer.

I was furious. And, I even felt like giving up.

Have you ever felt like a company was too big and you were too small to get any form of justice? If so, you can probably relate to this situation.

On the edge of giving up, I talked the situation over with a family member. That's when I resolved to speak up. I looked at the payment vendor's website and found the "Appeal" button. I clicked it and typed up my comment.

Will I prevail in this dispute with the online retailer? I don't know.

What counts is that I'm proud of myself for *not* giving up and for speaking up.

I realize that this may be a smaller issue—just about some

money.

But in the recent two days, I realized the important point: We had better get used to speaking up.

As I write this, the current man in the White House has been caught as an admitted sexual abuser.

Still, at this time, at least six men have been identified as sexual abusers. Some of them have lost their lucrative money-making deals and careers.

People are standing up and saying: We will NOT tolerate such abuse and oppression.

Wiccans Honor the Goddess

One of the reasons I like Wicca is: It gives women the power to run and lead their own lives—to be assertive and strong without any fear of ridicule or shaming.

In our community, we are strong Priestesses, and we have compassion and love for all. We are equally valued with the Priests of our spiritual path.

Wiccans Living in Society

I realize that many of us will not wear our faith out for all to see. (If you met me on the street, you would likely see my pentacle necklace.)

However, we, Wiccans, can support women who speak up.

When the powerful take advantage of the vulnerable, sometimes it is hard to fight and stand up to the powerful. The solution is to stand together.

We Need to Stand Up with the Women Who Call Out the Abuse

Have you noticed the systematic oppression of women? Think about it. If a woman reports abuse she is likely to lose her job and future opportunities. Some individuals say, "What are you talking about?" Consider this: How many employers want to hire a whistleblower?

If a man gets punched in the mouth, and he stands up, he is applauded.

If a woman gets sexually harassed, many individuals do what they can to shame her. They say, "You should have known better. You brought it on yourself."

We have been hearing in the news lately (at the time of this writing) about the men who took advantage of women working for them. This really angers me. I was sexually assaulted when I was young. I was afraid of being shamed. I was also afraid of being called a slut—and other forms of bullying perpetrated by my peers and society.

If you are a woman, you know what systematic oppression means—and how it feels to be harmed by it.

Progress Can Be Achieved

"It is better to light a candle than curse the darkness."
— *Eleanor Roosevelt*

Women created their own movement and worked for 72 years until women were granted their right to vote in the USA. The 19th Amendment to the U.S. Constitution was ratified by the states on August 18, 1920.

In April 2007, Wiccan U.S. soldiers gained the right to have a pentacle on their tombstones. This required a lawsuit. A plaintiff was Selena Fox, a Wiccan high priestess with Circle Sanctuary in Barneveld, Wisconsin.

During April 2007, U.S. Department of Veterans Affairs settled with Wiccans, so the pentacle was added to the list of 38 "emblems of belief" allowed on VA grave markers.

Progress Begins with You Today

Remember: Standing together we are more powerful than alone.

What small step can you do today to stand up against oppression?

Section Two:
Freedom to Express Yourself #2

How Do I Tell My Mainly Christian Friends/Family I'm Wiccan?

Are you considering the question of whether to go public with your Pagan faith?

Recently, one of my readers asked: "How do I tell my mainly Christian friends/family I'm Wiccan?"

"That's a vital and complicated topic," I thought. "Can I answer this in a brief article or would this be something to cover in half a book?"

Here's my answer to my reader:

Are you sure you need to go public with your Wiccan faith? Many Wiccans stay in the *broom closet* and are just happy with that. They have real and intense reasons to keep their faith private.

I have deep empathy for your situation—my own parents dragged my brother and me to their Christian church in our early years.

It's important to consider many issues before you do something that is irreversible.

1) You will lose some people.

Many Christians have been told by their religion-leaders that Wicca is evil. So, these Christians feel terror about Wicca. Doesn't it make sense that several people may react poorly to you telling them you have different beliefs than they do? You may be shunned—for a lifetime. Are you willing to lose some friends and family?

2) Are you ready to go public?

For many Wiccans, the cost of going public has been to lose their jobs and other opportunities because of their beliefs.

In this day of social media, several authors suggest: "There is no privacy."

Many of us have stories about how someone said, "I'll keep your secret," but later that person blurted out one's private information. How do you feel about the whole online world knowing that you are Wiccan?

3) Are you okay with the possible backlash?

Remember, many Christians have been misinformed about Wicca. Those individuals consider Wicca to be evil. How do some people treat those they consider evil? Have you seen the consequences of those who think they are righteous and they're only "punishing" evil-doers? People who are afraid tend to react in a rash manner.

After due consideration … here are some methods to express one's Wiccan faith publicly.

a) Let the other person start the conversation

I always wear a pentacle necklace. When some people see it, they make a comment. This opens the door for me to explain what the pentacle means. In this way, I'm able to share some of my beliefs and let them know some facts about the Wiccan spiritual path. (**Warning:** It depends on where you live. Since many Christians believe Wicca to be evil, you might open yourself to violence if you openly wear a pentacle. Please know that I live in Northern California where such an occurrence is unlikely.)

b) Start with common ground

"Margaret, I noticed that you're concerned about taking care of the environment," Amanda said. This is an example of starting with common ground. You can talk about how you also have a deep appreciation for nature. You can mention that walking in nature is like going to a sacred place for you. Some Wiccans mention that they have a "nature-focused religion."

Some people who believe in one God say that they have a feeling of awe when they see the Grand Canyon or a waterfall. The feeling of awe in the presence of nature can be common ground.

c) Talk about "The All" if that is part of your Wiccan Faith

Some Wiccans believe that "The All" began the universe. Then The All manifested as the Goddess who gave birth to the God ... and so forth.

A Christian might be able to understand "The All" as approximating what they view as "God, the Father."

d) Show Your Wiccan Faith in Action

Take up an environmental cause—if that fits for you. Here are options: Do cleanups in your neighborhood and demonstrate the positive things about your beliefs. Volunteer at an animal shelter or perform some other charitable work. In these ways, you demonstrate the life-enhancing actions that you do, inspired by your Wiccan faith.

Please do a lot of reflection. Get some advice from people you trust. Practice the actual words you will use for your tough conversations about your Wiccan faith ... if you decide to cross this irreversible threshold.

Section Two:
Freedom to Express Yourself #3

A Prayer to Give You Freedom

Do you have an issue that is dogging your heels? Maybe, it's a big decision—or a problem that you're having a hard time solving.

Sometimes, we just need to let go and know the God and Goddess have your best interests in mind.

Maria, a good friend, seems to be "clenched up" a lot of the time. She's actually losing energy.

I thought about a prayer that could help her "unclench."

Prayer to Release Yourself from an Attachment to an Outcome

I release myself from the outcome of _____.
May I have peace in my heart and comfort in my body while I let go of _____.

The God and Goddess protect me and are looking out for me.
They love me and help me with things such as _____.
I know in my whole being that all will be right about _____
For the God and Goddess walk beside me and guide me.
So mote it be.

Section Two:
Freedom to Express Yourself #4

How to Remember Your Dreams

Want to remember your dreams? Here is a chant to say aloud before you go to sleep at night.

Through wisps of clouds
On whispers of winds
My mind opens doorways
To secrets within.

Though wind howls
And shadows distract
My mind finds truth
The curtains pull back.

So mote it be!

Section Two:
Freedom to Express Yourself #5

Are the Gods Angry?

As you see the broadcast news or news reported online, are you empathizing with people running from Southern Florida to save their lives? (at the time of this writing)

Do you pause and ask what's going on here?

Hurricane Harvey wreaked havoc on Texas. Now, Hurricane Irma, while at Category 5, stomped Barbuda. Irma now stalks Southern Florida—soon to make landfall. Mexico just endured an earthquake, considered the worst in centuries.

Wiccans I know are getting impressions during meditation that the God and Goddess are upset.

Several experts suggest that global warming has a role in causing these severe hurricanes. Peter Spinks wrote, in his post, *Global Warming Changing Tilt of Earth's Spin Axis:* "Having once tilted towards Canada, the polar axis is now drifting towards Britain at roughly 16 centimeters a year, the NASA measurements reveal."

Some Wiccans suggest that the God and Goddess are showing their anger in how They are not moderating the devastation of hurricanes. The God and Goddess appear fed up with our pollution and carelessness for the Earth.

So, what can we do?

As witches, we are truly connected to our environment. We can feel the tides of the Earth changing. The seasons are not as they were before. As Peter Spinks mentioned, the earth is literally changing its axis.

Start with something simple.

Clean up our Great Mother whenever and wherever you can. Join the effort at litterproject.com. Or donate to help preserve the forests: conservation.org and animals: worldwildlife.org. Or pick another favorite organization.

Each of us can contribute to the efforts to undo the mess. We need to take responsibility for our actions.

As Wiccans, we have a connection to the God and Goddess. We can make amends and curb our destructive behavior.

We can actually deepen our connection with the God and Goddess. We can help Them in our efforts to take care of our home, the Earth.

Section Two:
Freedom to Express Yourself #6

The Hidden Truth About a Wiccan Incarnation

"I did not want to be in that car accident. Nothing you can say to me will change my mind," my friend, Rhonda, said. She was loud, real loud.

"Okay," my other friend, David, replied.

"Don't tell me that I chose what I wanted to happen in this incarnation—"

"I wasn't—"

"Don't say that there's some lesson in all this—"

"I didn't—"

"All right! What could be a lesson in all of this…?" Rhonda said, then she sat down. David just sat there for a moment or two. Just breathing. Just letting Rhonda calm down.

Some time ago, at a gathering of friends, David suggested that we make choices before we incarnate here on earth.

These choices give us challenging situations to help us learn certain lessons while we're here.

I once heard a speaker say, "If it's true that we make choices before we incarnate—maybe we better hope that we didn't say, 'I want to learn patience.' I could imagine a person in your soul group raising his hand. He says, 'I'll help you with that. I'll be your first husband.'"

As I was reflecting on this, I had a thought. A disturbing thought. What if I chose to go through the hardship of gaining weight, becoming obese, and then struggling to lose weight?

I chose this? NO!

Or maybe? Could it be that I planned to go through this weight-trouble, so I could learn empathy for others?

Wait a minute. Wasn't I already in the empathy-club?—with enduring the torture from my brother when we were kids. (I was a tiny girl when he held me down, drowning in a neighbor's swimming pool. There was more....)

Repeatedly, I hear about women who were attacked in their younger years, and they did something to get "bigger" or at least, to "be unattractive to male attention."

Author Roxane Gay was gang-raped when she was 12 years old. She writes in her book, *Hunger: A Memoir of (My) Body*, "I ate and ate and ate in the hopes that if I made myself big, my body would be safe. I buried the girl I was because she ran into all kinds of trouble. I tried to erase every memory of her, but she is still there, somewhere. . . . I was trapped in my body, one that I barely recognized or understood, but at least I was safe."

I have dropped 42 pounds. I've kept them off. To me, I think that bringing my Wiccan faith into the mix has helped.

Sure, I make certain to cast Circle and to gather with my coven.

I often do a candle-lighting ritual. (I certainly light a candle to say, 'thank you!' to Goddess Squat for parking spaces!)

But I've brought a Goddess Style* to my eating habits now. I'm on purpose with eating that which comes from the Goddess and dropping processed "food."

Every day, I eat natural plants (unprocessed) and natural animal protein (unprocessed).

The big change is that I keep processed sugar and carbs out of my diet as much as I can.

Here's my point: These changes have helped me in two ways: Get closer to my Gods and move forward with my healthy goal of weight loss.

42 pounds means a lot. I'll put it plainly. I've backed away from a dangerous weight. You see, my mother has diabetes. My efforts have kept me away from that health problem!

I'm grateful to God and Goddess for Their Support.

I've learned that as I take better care of myself and I connect with God and Goddess, I do NOT need the extra weight to feel safe.

After all the neglect and physical abuse in my childhood … I can now be free.

Wait! Let's pause here.

What a transformation!

What if I chose (on the spiritual plane before this incarnation) that I was going to take a journey in which I'd be hurt deeply, long for safety and then rise to have a new goal … to … be … FREE.

Is that what you want, my friend? To be free?*

* If you want to take great care of yourself related to weight loss, please consider my *online course, Goddess Style Weight Loss* at GoddessStyleWeightLoss.com.

Section Three:
Freedom to Be Healthy

The doctor handed me a sheet of paper. *Carcinoma.*
"Okay, it's cancer," I said.
The doctor sort of nodded. I thought, *What? You can't even say the word?*
I got that patch of skill removed. *I am healthy today.*
That's something to focus on.
Have you tried to lose weight? Did it you feel it was all about denying yourself of your favorite foods? It's almost as if "healthy" is about homework, housework, just about anything unpleasant.
This year, I dropped 42 pounds permanently.
One of things I've learned is that healthy is about "I feel better. Right now. This moment."
For me, losing weight is *not* about conforming to any media-driven stereotype of "beauty."
I'll take healthy.
How about you?
Do you want to feel better?

Imagine Goddess standing at your shoulder, saying, "You're worth it. I want to you to feel better. I want you to have more energy. I'll give you the strength to persevere. I will help carry your burdens. I'll give you that intuitive feeling about what to do next."

Section Three:
Freedom to Be Healthy #1

Wiccans and the Breath of Life of the Goddess

Have you felt alone or like you've hit bottom? Would you like to experience the Goddess's Breath of Life?

When do we really need the God's and Goddess's love and light?

Every day? Yes. And in particular, when you're feeling sick. I just had another coughing jag that almost split me in two. I keep reminding myself to let the Gods' love and light in.

Their healing breath of life can soothe and heal even the most broken parts of us.

When we look at the word *enthusiasm*, we realize the Latin origin of the word includes "theos (God)" and the meaning "inspired by God." *Inspire* means "breathe life into."

Three Common Blockages that Can Keep You from Receiving Goddess's Breath of Life

Here are Three Blockages you may experience:
- Distraction from Your Essence
- Feeling Unworthy
- Loss of Hope

1. Distraction from Your Essence

When I think of the meaning of "Your Essence," I think of Your True Self, which is what the God and Goddess meant for you to be. This concerns your True Path.

We all have a True Path in life. It consists of the lessons and goals we set up before we incarnated here on the physical plane.

If we're distracted from Our True Self, we can feel certain forms of pain. These can manifest as feelings of being alone and unworthy. These feelings create blockages to our True Path.

Many Wiccans connect with their natural state of peace and comfort while meditating, chanting or doing a ritual or breathing process.

2. Feeling Unworthy

With my blog, GoddessHasYourBack.com, I've shared part of my journey in dealing with symptoms of clinical depression. With these symptoms I can feel unworthy of love and kindness, even from the Gods!

So, how do we transform this feeling of unworthiness to happiness or even enthusiasm? Meditation is a great way to start on the road to the God and Goddess.

Many Wiccans find that focusing on the breath can be helpful, too. Here is an easy Breath Exercise to help remove blocks in your way to the Gods.

Breath Exercise
As you take in a long, slow breath, say silently,
"I breathe in Light and Goddess's Love."

As you breathe out slowly, say silently,
"I breathe out pain and distraction."

3. Loss of Hope

During the recent political events in the USA, many people feel hopeless. Then, something good happened. Recently, there was a big turnout of African-American women voters in Alabama. They voted to make sure an alleged-pedophile candidate did NOT get elected. (I feel he should *not* have been allowed to run in the first place.) This resulted in the first Democratic senator to be elected to represent Alabama in 25 years.

This positive outcome reminded me that we have a choice to focus on the good moments of life. In this way, we can nurture hope within our heart.

So, if you feel a loss of hope, see if you can find something good to focus on. This helps open the door so that you can receive the Goddess's Breath of Life.

Section Three:
Freedom to Be Healthy #2

Depression and Food—A Wiccan Solution

"Don't I deserve that cake?" I thought. "I worked so hard today, and I am so tired. I still have so much more to do! Besides, no one cares, anyway."

That last part is a depression-dripping comment. Having depression and trying to lose weight is a hard thing to do. Why? When you're depressed, you look to find comfort in any form you can. Food is an easy outlet for feeling safe and comforted when you're depressed. I should know: I have significant depression, and I have been fighting to lose weight for, at least, twenty years.

Why did I turn to food? When depressed, I looked for energy to do many things: To feel safe, to stay awake, and to stop feeling lonely.

In therapy for many years, I constantly worked on my self-esteem. During this process, I felt a big disappointment since I had gained so much weight. It was hard to feel good about myself.

I tried to lose weight many times. Joining a gym and even Weight Watchers at one point. Nothing worked….

Now, I have let go of 42 pounds. How did I do it? By turning to the God and the Goddess. I gratefully received Their gifts of vegetables, fruits of the earth, and Their love. I started to become the person They saw in me.

Before this, I only saw food as comfort. But now, I see food as fuel and something to be enjoyed in moderation. I see natural foods given by the Goddess as gifts to be savored and appreciated—not just gobbled down without thought or enjoyment.

1. Focus on the Gifts of the Goddess—A Simple Plan of Comfort During Weight Loss

Just imagine what the Goddess wants for you. She wants to give you health and happiness.

So, we begin with something simple: The Goddess gives us vegetables. I started eating vegetables for breakfast and ate natural proteins—not processed foods. And you know what? It worked! In the beginning, I dropped two pounds a week.

Now before you say, "YUCK!!! Vegetables for breakfast," hear me out.

You can get your veggies and natural protein in a simple way.

I emphasize simple (and requiring little energy) because a person suffering depression symptoms experiences low energy. For example, omelets are a good choice. You can scramble two eggs in a bowl and then cut up some onions, red bell peppers and even add some spinach. Sauté the veggies first in olive oil.

Then pour the eggs into another pan and begin cooking your omelet.

2. Bring Goddess into Your Cooking Routine

With deep gratitude, say aloud (while you're cooking):
Thank you, Goddess for Your Bounty.
I'm grateful for how You help me.

At a certain point, add the veggies to your omelet, even a little cheese for some added flavor.

There you go: A healthy breakfast. Try it, you may be surprised at how well it works.

3. Another Way to Get Your Greens in the Morning

Into a blender, toss in frozen berries, a fist full of spinach, a cup of non-fat or low-fat milk, and half a banana. Blend this mixture for a yummy shake. I call it the Green Monster. One of these is really filling and healthy for you, too.

4. Keep Things Simple and Be Conscious About How You Turn to the God and Goddess

I've shared some details about keeping one's food intake a simple process that requires a small amount of energy. I've noticed with my depression that my energy can be in short supply.

Now, I'll share something vital about turning to God and Goddess for comfort. Do not make it a big deal and a big production. By this, I mean, address God and Goddess simply. Above, I shared how to say a quick prayer while you're cooking.

Along this line, you could do a simple offering of a candle to the Goddess at dinner time.

You might imagine that "Depression says, 'You don't

have energy and you're not going to feel better."

Instead, by using simple prayers and simple healthy food preparation, you can get some real comfort from God and Goddess.

May Goddess give you great comfort.

Section Three:
Freedom to Be Healthy #3

Wicca and Healing Childhood Trauma

How is your health?

Researchers note how extreme and terrible childhood experiences can affect our health and journey throughout life.

If you endured abuse or neglect as a child, it is possible to heal, and Wicca can make a vital difference for you.

I've written about how Wicca empowered me to leave an abusive marriage.

How was I vulnerable to fall into an abusive marriage? As you can imagine, I had experienced a previous pattern of abuse—as a child.

Researchers refer to abuse and neglect that is inflicted on young people as Adverse Childhood Experiences (ACE).

I recently viewed a TED Talk by Dr. Nadine Burke Harris on the topic "How Childhood Trauma Affects Health Across a Lifetime."

In her work at a clinic in Hunters Point, San Francisco, Dr. Nadine observed that households had various elements that affected the children (including violence, neglect, substance abuse, family member incarceration, and more).

Dr. Nadine, in her TED Talk, noted that many of her medical colleagues in her audience would also respond that they had Adverse Childhood Experiences. Dr. Nadine concluded that this not just a problem in low social-economic neighborhoods. This is a nationwide health problem.

How Wiccans Can Heal

As Wiccans, we have tools to help us deal with stress we have now or the residual effects of childhood trauma. What are these tools?

1. Meditation

We can talk with the God and Goddess and ask for guidance.

2. Candle Magick

We can do candle magick to heal and create peace in our lives.

3. Chanting

We can chant and use our intense feelings to create positive change.

4. Prayer

We can ask the God and Goddess through meditation for Their help.

We can also open an internal dialogue with God and Goddess*

* You could simply begin with "Goddess, please help me heal and be free of trauma of my past. What can I do today to nurture myself?" At this point, wait and listen for internal guidance bestowed by the Goddess. You might get immediate guidance or receive Goddess' guidance some time later.

Learn to Shift When Helpless Feelings Arise

A major problem caused by Adverse Childhood Experiences is that we regress. We fall back into helpless feelings that were natural to feel as a child.

We, as Wiccan adults, can now be the kind caregivers we did not have.

You can, with help from God and Goddess, take much better care of yourself now.

The point is to not stay in helpless feelings you felt while you were traumatized as a child. These feelings of overwhelm are still relevant today—perhaps, even in this moment for you. Remind yourself of MCCP (meditation, candle magic, chanting and prayer). Help yourself shift out of feelings of overwhelm.

Remember, it is possible to heal!

P.S. If you're curious about you own ACE score, you could take a related quiz. (You can find the quiz via Google.)

If you note that you have a significant score, take action to care for yourself.

I found that my score is "4." I do a lot to stay stronger and healthier (including support from a therapist, doctors, my husband, family, friends, exercise, Wiccan Rituals to connect with God and Goddess … and more).

What do you need to heal and stay strong, my friend?

Section Three:
Freedom to Be Healthy #4

The Flame Within You

"Ahhh. My throat's on fire and my ears hurt," my friend, Sharon, said when describing how sick she felt.

Her comment inspired me to think about how, at this time, many of us are having our internal flame diminished.

How can we stoke and tend the flame within?

Getting a cold, having allergies or just feeling shut away from the light of the Gods can really be a downer. This is when we need to feed the fire within.

Doing ritual can help us keep our internal flame lit.

"With the discovery of fire-making, ritual may have started. You did this and this, and up sprang the magickal flame, a spirit at your command." – Gerald B. Gardner

Consider the Element Fire. As humans learned to harness the benefits of fire, we discovered an essential part of our rituals. What rituals can we do to keep our flame roaring not just a weak glow?

Here are three things you can do to keep your flame bright and powerful:

1. Walk in the Wild

Recently, I've seen materials from doctors mentioning ecotherapy. Ecotherapy is defined as "exposure to nature and the outdoors as a form or component of psychotherapy." (yourdictionary.com)

Witches have long known that nature is good for us. Now, doctors have finally started to catch on.

I love walking in nature. Why? Because plants, trees, and water around us take in the toxins and free a person from such toxins. Because I deal with symptoms of clinical depression, I walk in nature to become free of sadness, anxiety, and fear found in my body and soul. This does help me. Getting a thorough cleaning and being close to the God and Goddess always brings me joy.

The doctors may not yet know the true reasons why walking in nature is beneficial, but we, witches, know how it works.

For city dwellers, at least, talk a walk on a street decorated with living trees or walk in a public park.

2. Read Wiccan Books

Make reading a natural part of your day. Support your inner flame by reading in the direction your curiosity takes you.

At this dark time of the year, many Wiccans refrain from doing active magick.

What you can do is to immerse yourself in Wiccan education. (I believe in this and I created an online course *Goddess Style Weight Loss*.)

How do you make reading a ritual? Pick a certain place and a certain time. You could light a candle, sit down with a nice cup of tea, and read … and smile.

3. Meditate and Enter a Good Place—In This Moment

Wiccans use meditation to connect with all that is good in this moment. Focusing on your breath can be part of your gratitude-ritual. You are grateful for every breath of life—the gift from God and Goddess.

Here is a pattern:
Breathe in.
I stoke the Flame of Life.
Breathe out.
I breathe out all stress and strife.

A Bonus Idea: Meditation can also kindle your positive anticipation for future good things. Think of what you would like to work on next year. Write down your thoughts on separate slips of paper and then place each item, one at a time, on your altar and meditate on how you want to accomplish the different goals.

You can light a candle and play some soft, relaxing music in the background.

In summary, I invite you to keep your internal flame bright and powerful.

Remember:
- Walk in the Wild
- Read Wiccan Books
- Meditate and Enter a Good Place—In This Moment

Section Three:
Freedom to Be Healthy #5

A Ritual Bath: Step into Relief

Do certain stories in the current news leave you feeling burdened? A ritual bath can provide the refreshing feeling you long for.

You can add a potion pod to your ritual bath. A potion pod is a custom-made ice cube that melts in the water of a ritual bath.

1. Brew a potion for a ritual bath

You can brew a strong potion with herbs and flowers. Make a brew for cleansing.

Warning: Be sure to use only herbs and flowers that are "food-safe." The idea is for your body to only absorb energies that enhance your health.

You might consider adding ingredients to your potion pod that can help you banish bad luck or negative energy.

2. Fill your ice cube tray

Fill your tray(s) with your brew. You can use several trays for different brews.

3. Freeze the potion in an ice cube tray

Place your tray into the freezer and let your brew solidify. Once the cubes have frozen, break them out of the ice cube tray, place them into a container, and label it with the contents and the date.

4. Place a potion pod in your ritual bath water and use a fresh towel

Be sure to thoroughly wash any trays after use.

When you're ready for a ritual bath, place one to three potion pods into your hot bath water. The pods will melt, letting the brew infuse the bath water. Be sure to use a fresh towel for drying off after your ritual bath.

When you use this process, you will have your potion pods pre-made for when you want to take a ritual bath.

May this process bring you comfort and peace.

Section Three:
Freedom to Be Healthy #6

Dealing with Depression While Having Cancer

"You okay, Moonwater? Are you sick?" my friend, Lisa, asked.

"I don't know. The doctor took some skin from near my wrist. I'm waiting on a biopsy," I replied.

Then, the next day, the doctor's office left a voicemail for me—a vague message.

But such a fast return call promised bad news. I had to wait the whole weekend until I could get someone on the phone. The answer was … cancer.

Now the question was … did they cut away all the cancerous cells? The afflicted spot was the size of a dime, and the doctor had used a dermablade to cut away a nickel-sized area.

Again—it was about waiting to find out.

Can you relate? Have you had anxiety waiting for news

related to something you had no control over?

Let's add depression to the mix of anxiety and cancer.

My depression symptoms already pushed me to see a bleak future. Now, with the cancer-diagnosis, my mind spiraled into dark corners. Fear, dread, pain.

So, what can we do to sooth these feelings?

Here are Three Practical Ways to Soothe Feelings of Dread:

1. Talk with Friends

You can circle the wagons with your friends/family.

You'll want to be selective about with whom you share your difficult news. I even have a kind friend who prefers texting to talking on the phone. We had a good conversation.

Still, many of us find talking on the phone or visiting in-person to be more helpful.

Many times, your friends and family can be supportive and give you strength. This includes your coven mates if you are in a coven.

A select number of your friends can and will support you. You can lean on them when life gets tough.

Certain friends helped me see the light when depression only showed darkness.

My husband gave me a different perspective. He called the operation a "cancer event." (I didn't like this phrase.)

His point was that the operation was likely successful. So, the situation was over (like an event). He added, "Until the data is in, it's good." By this he meant, if you don't have an indication otherwise, carry on as if you're going to get good news. Sometimes, he calls it "postponing worry that might prove unnecessary."

Some people may find this perspective useful at times.

One thing I like about my husband's comment is that it's about holding a positive thought and sending that positive thought as energy into the universe.

2. Pray to the God and Goddess

I talked a lot to the God and Goddess. I asked Them to postpone my worries until I had more information. They sat with me in my fear and comforted me. They quieted my fears.

I said, "Please let this be okay. Give me guidance. Let me have the strength to go through this situation." I focused on these intentions with the God and Goddess. This provided me a whole different direction than my depression symptoms would have brought to me.

So, when you have a serious question with no answer and you feel anxious, talk to the God and Goddess. See if you feel a subtle shift inside. That would be the God and Goddess providing you subtle support.

3. Perform a Ritual

Do a simple candle ritual to calm and reassure yourself.

I find lighting a candle and asking for peace/faith/comfort really helps me.

You can say:
With this Candle
I honor You, God and Goddess
Please fill me with Light.
Lend me Your Might.
So Mote It Be.

May these above practices bring you comfort and healing.

Section Three:
Freedom to Be Healthy #7

Chant to Keep You Strong

Here is a chant to keep you strong:

Lord and Lady,
Make me strong.
Others oppress,
And I hold on.
You give me strength
All others may blink.
My worth is Your Blessing
My joy is Your Blessing
So Mote It Be.

I hope we can all stand tall for wisdom, kindness, and compassion.

Section Three:
Freedom to Be Healthy #8

Keep Up My Strength Chant

For those of us who seek better health in the process of dropping excess weight:

Keep Up My Strength Chant

Power by the Silver Moon
Persistence is the great boon.
Losing weight that had cocooned,
My beauty had been consumed.
The Beauty that is me,
Step Forward Now.
Oh, how lovely You are Now.

Section Three:
Freedom to Be Healthy #9

How to Revitalize Your Wiccan Practice

"What do you do when you go through a rough patch and your Wiccan rituals don't bring you peace, like they used to?" my friend, Amanda, asked me.

I pondered this for a while. One idea that arose is: "Do something positive that is outside your routine."

What is your routine?

When I think of my own routine, I realize that I get up, handle email—and at some point, in the day I take a walk with my husband. Certainly, I seek out my cat, Magick. He gets scratched and petted. Then, he comes back for more. I do some writing.

Sometimes, your daily life needs a little pick-me-up. When I can, I like to get my hair done—I do need help to maintain my purple shade of hair. I enjoy the attention, and I relax while the stylist does my hair. Afterward, I feel refreshed and ready to go!

The same can be true for your Wiccan practice.

Pick a time to make a date with yourself and the God and Goddess. Pamper yourself in ritual, give the Gods offerings and tell Them how much you love Them. Some might ask, "Pamper myself?" How about a luxurious ritual bath?

You know what your Gods like. Give Them such an offering and create a simple ritual around that offering.

For example, you could have an in-home spa night when you provide offerings to the Gods made of Their preferences. Then during the ritual, you can soak in a nice warm tub infused with herbs, while you bask in candle light.

Relax with a glass of your favorite beverage and your favorite food. Talk to the Gods, tell Them how much you appreciate Them watching over you. Listen... breathe... relax...

Break your routine. If you tend to stay in-doors, perhaps, you'd enjoy taking a walk next to a body of water. Several creative people mention that they get inspired when next to water. As you walk, breathe deeply and thank God and Goddess.

These are just a few ways to inject new life into your Wiccan practice.

Section Four:
Freedom for Abundance

I opened the envelope. At 17, with my first job, I looked at the first check of my life. *Oh…wow… I made this money. And it is mine!*

Imagine that Goddess says about any income you receive, "It's yours. And there's more for you."

What a feeling of abundance!

By the way, **each time you take a moment to be *grateful* for any form of abundance you experience, you guide the universe to give you more.** The universe sees that you're grateful and says, "You're a good steward of what you have, and I will give you more."

What gets in the way of our abundance? A mindset of lack. Perhaps, you've heard about that.

Here's where Wiccans have an advantage. We can do rituals. We can call on the Goddess directly.

I even wrote about this. In my book, *Beyond the Law of Attraction to Real Magick*, I came right out and said it: "To put it simply, the Law of Attraction is a form of magick, but people who read an introductory book on the Law of Attraction are often denied enough information to truly make the Law of Attraction work in their own lives. So, to really make a positive difference in your life, we need to talk about real magick."

Let's get started.

Section Four:
Freedom for Abundance #1

When You Really Need Money— a Wiccan Ritual

"What is going on? I have so many spiritual friends who are having trouble with money," my friend, Sabrina, said.

Wiccans do have possibilities to use magick to ease their burdens.

Here is a ritual to increase your money flow. Do this ritual on the waxing moon, for a duration of seven days (before the moon is full). If you can start on a Sunday, even better.

Financial Abundance Ritual

What you will need:
- Green 7-day knobbed candle
- Candle Snuffer
- Candle holder
- Money Drawing Oil*
- $100 bill (if necessary you can use $10)
- Altar Pentacle
- Money Drawing Incense**

- Charcoal for burning incense
- Altar
- Ritual tools
- Cakes
- Wine/juice

*Money Drawing oil
- 1 drop Cinnamon oil
- 3 drops Ginger oil
- 5 drops Flax Seed oil

Combine all three oils in a carrier oil such as jojoba oil. Let the combined oil sit in the moonlight for three days. Allow it to stand in the dark for three weeks. Do not let it sit in the sun.

**Money Drawing Incense
- 3 parts Cinnamon
- 2 parts Ginger
- 3 parts Flax Seed
- 2 parts Myrrh

Mix ingredients with mortar and pestle, and let the mixture sit for three days before doing the ritual. Do not let it sit in the sun.

When the time is right, begin your ritual.

Cast circle in the usual manner.

Cleanse and consecrate your candle and the $100 bill. Dress your candle by rubbing the Money Drawing Oil from the tip to the base. Next rub a small amount of the Money Drawing Oil on your $100 bill and place it on your altar pentacle while saying:

Money Chant
Money comes
Money flows
Money stays
Money comes to me
Only in positive ways
And grows and grows!

Place the candle in the candle holder. Place them on top of your $100 bill. Repeat the Money Drawing Oil chant three more times, while concentrating on the candle.

Envision seeing your wallet/purse stuffed with money. Envision being able to pay bills and getting the things you need and want.

When you feel you have this image firmly in your mind, light the candle. Keep concentrating and focusing on your goal until the first knob has been consumed. Snuff your candle with a candle snuffer. **Caution:** Do *not* blow out your candle. This will blow out your intention.

For six more days in a row, repeat lighting the candle and focusing on your intention—with each knob. Once you have finished all seven days and the candle burns itself out, take the $100 bill and place it in your purse or wallet. Carry the bill to attract more money. Once you have what you desire, give the bill to charity***.

May this help you on your financial abundance journey.

*** **An Important Consideration:** Sometimes, a person needs to do more than one ritual. Why? Because he or she has significant blocks. If the ritual doesn't work the first time, you may have to directly address your personal blocks to financial abundance.

Section Four:
Freedom for Abundance #2

Money Spell for Your Inner Peace — and to Help Others

Hurricane Harvey has carved a path of devastation (at the time of this writing), leaving many people homeless and suffering. Several Wiccan friends have expressed their concern about not having money to make donations to ease the victims' suffering.

If you're enduring a financial hardship, here is a simple spell so you can send a blessing of energy in lieu of money.

With this Money Attraction Spell, you can create a "magickal check" (on virgin paper). The point is that you are using this magickal check as a symbol that will draw the energy of the Universe to the benefit of the victims of Hurricane Harvey's devastation.

What you will need:
- "Your Magickal Check" [you will write it up to

appear like a regular check from your checkbook)
- Money oil
- Green candle
- Candle holder
- Quill
- Dragon's blood ink
- Ritual tools
- Cakes and Wine
- Dragon's blood incense
- Cast Circle in the usual manner.

Cleanse and consecrate your candle and magickal check with your holy water. Charge the candle and magickal check with the dragon's blood incense smoke. Dress your candle from wick to base with your money oil.

Dip your quill into the dragon's blood ink to draw up your magickal check. Write down an amount of money that you want to go to a particular disaster-related charity.

Say:
This money to you
To help soothe all your woes.

Place the magickal check on your pentacle and put your hands on it. Concentrate on money flowing to the victims of the disaster. See them getting the vital things they need: fresh water, food, dry clothes and warm beds. Focus these thoughts into the magickal check.

Place the candle in the candle holder and set them on top of your magickal check.

Channel energy into the candle and magickal check. When you feel the candle and magickal check are charged to your liking, light the candle and chant:

Money, money go their way,

Help give comfort, save their day.
Money in and their suffering out,
Clean up this disaster all about.
Safety and kindness, will you give,
Let love, and human kindness live.
So swiftly go to all that need you,
End this pain, let the Gods be with you.

Make sure to let the candle burn all the way down until it is completely extinguished. (Be sure to avoid leaving a candle unattended, while it is burning.)

Do your Cakes and Wine Ceremony.
Close Circle.

May this ritual ease your heart and help the victims of Hurricane Harvey's devastation.

Section Four:
Freedom for Abundance #3

The Wiccan Path to Let Go—and to Invite New Energy and Abundance In

"My home has exploded,' Mary said.
"What?!" I asked.
"My place is getting new windows and there is sooo much stuff to move!" she said. "I really need to start letting go of things. Even things that have a hold on my heart." She sighed.

Are you inundated with an overwhelming number of things in your home? Need to pare it down a little?

Just like Mary, I can do with less clutter in my home. So, this weekend I'm doing a major paring down of my belongings.

If you're called to clear out some clutter, here are some helpful ideas.

Ask yourself:

Have I used this item in the past twelve months? If the

answer is *no*, then you can donate it or recycle it.

Hold an item in your hands and ask, "Does this truly make me happy?" If so, keep it. If you have a so-so feeling, then chuck it.

Look at an item and consider whether you could sell it on the Internet or at a garage sale.

I'm using these ideas as a guideline this weekend. I'm noticing that I need to have enough energy to tackle this big process.

Here is a simple chant to help in the process.

Get Rid of Things Chant
E-ho eee and E-ho wo
Help me get this stuff to go!
Clutter, clutter go away,
Never, ever come my way.
As you shrink, my space expands,
Throughout my home, no junk may land.
So bye, bye, and never come back,
Goddess, get my grace on track.

One of my mentors noted that when we let go of stuff, we open the door for more peace, grace, and abundance to flow to us.

Section Four:
Freedom for Abundance #4

Recover Something Precious

Have you ever lost something precious? Here is a chant to help you find what was lost.

My precious thing
Whether stolen or lost in time.
My precious thing
Gods bring back to me what is mine.
My precious thing
Return now so I can feel fine.

So mote it be!

Section Five:
Freedom to Be Creative

"That's perfect!" my friend, Rebecca, said, gushing over my design for a t-shirt. It had exactly what she wanted. It had a logo for a ten-year anniversary. The small animals that I had incorporated into the design were among the cutest things I'd ever drawn.

Oooooh! I enjoyed being creative—and having my design hit the spot!

If I asked you, "Are you creative?" you might say, "No. I don't draw. I don't write."

I invite you to realize that you're creative every day.

A friend of mine had to respond to someone asking, "How do you like my hair?"

She said, creatively, "I'm not used to it yet."

You might ask, "How was that creative?"

It was better than. "Ack! It's awful. What were you thinking?!"

Imagine Goddess saying, "Yes. You're creative. That's what you're meant to be. I'll keep giving you little

nudges — little intuitive thoughts and feelings."
Then, we're charged with getting out of our own way.

"Keep pure your highest ideal; strive ever toward it; let naught stop you or turn you aside. For mine is the secret door which opens upon the Land of Youth; and mine is the Cup of the Wine of Life, and the Cauldron of Cerridwen, which is the Holy Grail of Immortality." – from The Charge of The Goddess *by Doreen Valiente (writing in the voice of the Goddess)*

What is the first step? Pause. Take a look. What can be your highest ideal? Did you like writing poetry in high school? Do you want to try it again?
Let Goddess hold you in safety as you try new things.
I tried yoga. Not a match.
Walking every day. That's a match.
I tried oil painting. Can't do that, anymore.
Digital painting. That works well.
You get the picture.
What's a big benefit of creativity? Sometimes, you get this wonderful feeling of comfort. *Yes, I have an ability with this. Goddess gave me that.*
What might the Goddess be calling you to?

Section Five:
Freedom to Be Creative #1

How You Can Interweave Wicca with Your Daily Life

Savvy Wiccans learn to interweave their practice in the spare moments of daily life.

1. **Read and study during your lunch break.**

You can bring your e-reader or book wherever you go. If you're uncomfortable about people seeing the cover of your paperback book, use some paper and make a simple cover. Study during your breaks during the day.

Catching five minutes and ten minutes here and there can keep you on track to grow in the Craft.

2. **Take five minutes in the morning for the God and Goddess.**

Meditation is a great way to start the day. Communicating with the Gods and checking in with Them can keep you on your track for a closer bond with Them. It's important to keep the lines of communication open with the Gods. Even a five-minute meditation session can make a real difference.

3. When cooking, choose foods based on their magickal benefits.

Many of us cook daily, anyway. So, it's a good idea to enhance your Wiccan practice with how you make good choices about the foods you eat.

For example, if you're looking for love, cook a meal using basil. Basil can be used for attracting wealth, too. Talk about a double-benefit!

Need protection, try garlic. Make some garlic bread to go with pasta. Many Wiccans use garlic for healing, too. Consider adding garlic to chicken soup for a wonderful taste. This works well for healing from colds and flus.

Create your own cooking style.

4. Take a daily walk around trees.

Even just a ten-minute walk can give you an experience of communing with nature and feeling the healing from the Gods.

Walking around in nature helps scrub your aura. Furthermore, such a walk drains negative energy out of your body. No wonder doctors have started prescribing walking in nature—now called "ecotherapy."

In summary, here is an example of how Laura incorporates Wiccan practice in her daily life. She wakes up 10 minutes early and gets in her 5-minute meditation. She walks in a park while listening to a Wiccan audio book during her break. She eats her "prosperity soup" during her lunchbreak.

As we've discussed: There are numerous ways to weave your magickal life into your mundane one.

Section Five:
Freedom to Be Creative #2

How You Can Change and Release Yourself from Being Stuck—A Wiccan Solution

Have you had moments, like me, of thinking, "Change is hard."

I like this quote:

"Magic is natural. It is a harmonious movement of energies to create needed change." – Scott Cunningham

This idea "magic is natural" can transform how you look at change.

Recently, I realized that the path of "harmonious movement of energies to create needed change" is a path that focuses on the pentagram and the 4 Elements plus Spirit.

As Wiccans we can use the Elements in magick to help us.

Each Element is a step toward change.

In the process, each Element serves as a step to the next one.

Air

The first step for making real change relates to the Element Air. Air represents thought. We need to know that we truly want to change in the first place.

Wanting change is *not* enough. To create real change, we must know that change is needed in our life. This knowing helps us make a real commitment.

Simply wishing for change does not get you where you need to go.

Begin with the idea and firm it up. An idea is a powerful thing. Just like a seed has the potential to grow into a beautiful rose, an idea can manifest into something great.

A well-formed idea includes specifics. You want a target that is sharp like a tack. Something you can measure and see. I will use my weight loss of 42 lbs. as an example during this post.

In January (of this writing), I reflected on how my doctor told me I needed to lose the weight one week earlier. Now, usually just telling someone to lose weight doesn't work. They need to *really want* to lose the weight. They need to make space for a permanent change in their life. So where could I begin?

Meditation served as my starting point.

Try it. Burn some incense and meditate on your idea. (By the way, burning incense relates to the Element of Air.)

During meditation, let your mind flow. Ultimately, you take that vague idea you have and shape it into a solid idea.

Losing weight was too vague of a target for me. So, I brought it down to a solid number. I wanted to lose five pounds. That's it. Just five pounds. It's something small, measurable, and it can be recorded by tracking my weight on a scale.

Fire

Having a firm idea is a good start. But you need the Element of Fire to get your will into the process. Fire helps give you that push, that extra oomph.

Fire gives you the passion to fulfill your idea.

Use passion to help you form a plan of action. For example, my plan was to focus on dropping five pounds. Using the passion of Fire, I did a **Weight Loss Spell:**

What you will need:
- One seven knob, green candle
- Banishing oil
- Candleholder
- Lighter

Warning: Be sure to do this spell during the waning moon.

Cast the Circle.

Cleanse and consecrate the oil and candle. Set the candle in its holder. Sit and meditate on your losing weight. See the candle as a representation of the excess weight. When you're ready, light the candle and say three times:

Little knobbed candle of green,
With powers, great and unseen.
I light you in the vast darkness so,
Illuminate health for me to know.
Bad eating habits and lethargy, I rip out
Of my life within and without!
Let this my prayer be answered now!

I pray that you will, I pray that you must,
For me to lose weight high water or bust!
As you my little green candle melts,
So too does my weight and waistline melt.
So mote it be!

Now sit and meditate on losing weight until the first knob is burned completely. Then put out the candle with a snuffer.

Repeat above spell for the next six days.

Do the Cakes and Wine Ceremony.
Close the Circle.

Taking action is a great step. Next, you'll need to marshal positive emotion.

Water
The Element of Water is associated with emotion. We've progressed from idea to passion to a plan of action.

Now, let's be sure that you keep yourself emotionally healthy during the process.

Losing five pounds was all and good, but I could derail my efforts if I drove myself nuts trying to be perfect. To take care of myself emotionally, I created a tool for myself—the Goddess Style Weight Loss method.

Take your plan of action and make a tool/method to help you emotionally.

Consider:

A weekly meeting with a friend to "rally the troops" and to keep you strong and consistent in your efforts

A *pamper yourself day* to help keep you calm. Or one

simple, nurturing action just for you: like getting a massage once a week.

Consider the possibility of getting pastoral counseling from a fellow Priest or Priestess. Your fellow Priest or Priestess has a unique insight into your journey as a Pagan. This can be especially helpful. Doing a ritual together can be just what's needed to have you move forward faster.

In some cases, working with a therapist related to emotional healing can help you stay on track. You may not realize that a past trauma may be influencing your behavior. I found that working with a therapist helped me deal with details from my past.

Earth

Stay grounded through the Element of Earth.

Part of grounding is to keep silent about your plans when in the presence of naysayers. Guard your energy against intrusions by naysayers, who can ruin one's magick work.

Imagine that you ground your plan of action into reality. Take the seed of your plan and plant it in the earth.

Let your seed of intention grow strong and create the change you desire.

At the core of Wicca—it is a joyous union with nature. The Earth is a manifestation of divine energy. – Scott Cunningham

This leads right into Spirit.

Spirit

Spirit is an essential facet of your journey to create positive change.

With Air, Fire, Water, and Earth, you have stepped into a new life. You're using the tools of change.

The last step is Spirit in which you manifest a permanent, positive change.

"If that which thou seekest thou findest not within thee, thou wilt never find it without thee." – written in the voice of the Goddess (found in The Charge of The Goddess by Doreen Valiente)

Your Spirit is within you, always. Your Spirit is your true connection with the God and Goddess.

Change fundamentally comes from within. When we do our magick and create change, we don't necessarily change the outer world, but we really change our inner world.

So, what do you want to change in your life?

Section Five:
Freedom to Be Creative #3

How You Can Overcome "Fences" in Your Life—A Wiccan Approach

Do you have fences in your life, keeping you from doing the things you really want to do? Maybe, they keep you from doing ritual on a regular schedule? Perhaps, they keep you from meditating daily.

How do we remove such blocks to our success in doing what we want?

Do as the Goddess says, as revealed in Doreen Valiente's poem, *The Charge of The Goddess:*

"Keep pure your highest ideal; strive ever toward it; let naught stop you or turn you aside."

You might say, "Well, that sounds nice, but how can I take a concrete step in that direction?"

Start with Your Highest Ideal

You need a target. What might you aim for?

We, as Wiccans, want to have a daily connection with God and Goddess.

There you go! We now have a Highest Ideal to aim for.

Take the Smallest Step toward Your Highest Ideal

What is the smallest step you can take to help you have a daily experience with God and Goddess?

Here are some suggestions:

1. Go on a daily walk in nature

Going for a walk in nature helps you connect with the God and Goddess. It's also a good form of exercise that can be done by most individuals. (With any form of exercise, check with your doctor.)

Set an alarm on your phone or watch to remind you to meditate on a regular basis (even if it's just three minutes a day)

When you hear the alarm ring, you know it is time for you to meditate. You might step to a backroom (or even a bathroom stall) and meditate for three minutes. Some years ago, one of my friends used to bring a chair to a balcony during his break at work. He would practice deep breathing and meditating for a few minutes—on that balcony. "It helped," he told me.

2. Set up a trigger to inspire you into action

You can set a candle on the dining table that you see on entering your apartment. You'll be reminded to set down your stuff and jacket and do a brief ritual before you move forward with your evening. In essence, you set a positive trigger (the candle) for yourself.

If you live alone or with someone who supports your Wiccan path, you can set up your altar the night before so when you get home the next day, it is already up and waiting for you.

Pre-setting your materials makes it much easier to get into action and do ritual instead of the default pattern of flopping down on the couch to watch TV.

Using a candle to get me started, I find that once I get into motion, I feel lots of energy that I didn't feel moments before. In this way, I actually complete some candle magick (for example).

3. Set up a weekly call with a friend about your conversation with the God and Goddess

Perhaps, you set up something called an Accountability Plan. You have a weekly call with a friend, and you both give a "progress report" on what you did that week to honor and be close with the God and Goddess.

When I use an Accountability Plan, I find that I do what I planned. Because I want to avoid talking about a failure to do ritual, I actually get it done during the week.

May these methods be helpful to you on your Wiccan Journey.

Section Five:
Freedom to Be Creative #4

The Wiccan's Solution for Doing What You Don't Feel Like Doing

Laundry! Paperwork! These are banes of my existence. (Okay, there are other difficult things, too …)

How can an exhausted Wiccan perk up and get difficult tasks done? (I'm talking about those tasks that we meet with procrastination!)

Candle Magic to Get into Action
Light a red candle and say:
The red candle glows,
My energy grows.
My ease now flows.
Completing this task,
Will be fast.
I will be free at last.

May this process help you.

Section Six:
Freedom to Be Me

When was the last time you felt free to be yourself?

Do you have certain friends with whom you can cut loose?

Sometimes, I wonder about social media. Do people need to use it as a garbage can to merely complain and be snarky? Is that what they think of as "free to be me" under the cover of an avatar?

What about "Free to Be Me" as a chance to express what's positive in your soul? Your gifts from Goddess. And, your quirky parts.

I admit it. I've got this thing about food. I must eat one thing on my dinner plate first—then I go onto the next item.

Does my family go, "Oh, that's so endearing"? Not really.

Still, I'm free to be me. In all my quirky glory. (Not really glory, but you get the idea).

Sometimes, I think about "Free to Be Me" as a time to express your True Self. It makes you feel good. Who is my True Self? It's when I'm courageous.

Those times I'm stuck in fear or discouragement is *not* the real me. That's just certain patterns.

But the first time, I geared up my courage to be a guest speaker in front of college students (a Comparative Religion class), *that* was the real me.

How about you? When have you expressed your True Self?

When have you expressed courage?

Have you noticed that when you really express yourself, it makes you feel good?

Imagine Goddess saying, "That's what I made you for. To show your brilliance."

Section Six:
Freedom to Be Me #1

The Wiccan Secret to Really Enjoying Your Life

Ever hear someone say something that just sticks with you?

A mentor of mine said, "If you don't devote yourself to the seasons in your life, you could let yourself fall into needless misery."

At the time, I thought I got what he meant. Since that time, some other ideas have risen in my thoughts.

The Time of Harvest Is Here

As witches know, Mabon is one of three seasons of harvest. Mabon just passed (as I wrote this), and we are reaping the bounty of the earth with all its produce. But it's not just the bounty of the earth that we can be harvesting at this time.

Several Wiccans I know sowed magick spells at earlier times this year. It's as if the multiple sessions of doing spells were like tending one's garden. Wiccans traditionally start in the Spring and work on our magickal goals at that time. Working and watching until Fall, we see how all our hard work pays off.

Recently, I have been doing just that, harvesting. I've experienced a major shift personally, and it has invigorated how I serve others, too.

January 1st (as of this writing), I started a new lifestyle with how I eat, connect with the Goddess and let go of excess weight. I let go of 36.8 lbs. permanently, and this journey inspired my book this year titled *Goddess Style Weight Loss*.

Later, I was up to 42 lbs. dropped from my body. And I realized that many of my circle would do even better with five weeks of support through my having an Online Course *Goddess Style Weight Loss*.

Here's a Secret: Start where you are. Start with what your heart and what the Gods call you to do.

On January 1st, I just focused on opening a new chapter of life for me—for my own health. Now, God and Goddess are guiding me to expand how I help others.

What About You? What New Chapter Awaits You in Life?

Let's come back to the idea of seasons. January was not a season for me to consider new projects. January was the season for me to take care of my health. Realize there are seasons in which we sow seeds, tend the garden, and later enjoy the harvest. Certainly, you'll need to plant for new growth at some point, too.

Sadness and Feeling of Depression without Your Passion

Perhaps, you're in a season in which sadness feelings are more visible.

Some people make their lives tougher. How? They have a lamentable story: "Oh, I don't feel passion in my life. Passion is for other people. You know—all those movie stars, best-selling authors, business people. I'm just somebody who's trying to get through the day."

It's just a story, my friend.

Reach out to the God and Goddess. You do *not* need to make a production of it. The God and Goddess greet you in whatever season you find yourself in.

An important point: Your Seasons may not follow the calendar year.

The God and Goddess guided me this year.

Some years ago, I didn't know the God and Goddess. My depression symptoms ran my life. I had no passion. I was unhappy and lost in my emotions. Having nothing to reach for, I spiraled and sank deeper into the land of sadness, loneliness, and self-hate.

Then, I began a process of studying books on Wicca, meditating and conducting ritual as a solitary witch. Things shifted into a higher gear when I joined a coven.

You see, I am passionate about my relationship with the God and Goddess. They are now such an intricate part of my life. When I found the Gods, things changed. And I started to sow new life into my existence.

Having some passion in my life kept me from spiraling out of control.

I invite you to dive in and engage with your Wiccan practice. Find some passion for yourself.

Happiness Can Rise at Any Time—It's Not Like Waiting for Summer

Remember, as a child, being desperate for the school year to end? Come on, Summer! Twenty minutes left of the last class. What's wrong with that clock! The big hand is not moving!

Some of us live as if happiness is this unknown island in the mist of the future.

What is happiness? Surely, it's different for different people.

I've learned, for me, it's appreciating some cozy moments of each day.

Perhaps, the problem is: Many of us are looking for a fictional time when everything goes smoothly.

Instead …

A friend shared with me a quote:

"We do not remember days, we remember moments."
– Cesare Pavese

I invite you to reach to the God and Goddess and to develop more happy moments in each day.

The God and Goddess give us all sorts of opportunities throughout the whole year. So, don't be shy on grabbing them. Keep in mind that the Gods are helping you by offering you opportunities to grow. Also, some opportunities don't look like opportunities. Then come in the clothes of trouble or even hardship. But they will help you grow.

Remember, each of us lives in seasons: time to sow, to tend the garden, and to enjoy the harvest.

So, don't let opportunities slip away. Grab them!

Grab them and follow your bliss.

Section Six:
Freedom to Be Me #2

A Wiccan Walks a New Path

Do you ever think about how God and Goddess made everything? You look at a tree and you say, "That works." You look at a waterfall, and you might say, "Ahhh, beautiful."

"How about a diet?" my husband asked me.

"No! Humans made diets!" I said.

No wonder, diets don't work. Why? I've noticed that a diet seems to be so much about punishment.

There's a Myth that you can punish yourself into doing something good. Here's what I discovered: I try to be good and eat only what is on the diet. And when I fail? I feel guilt that I wasn't strong enough or good enough. I even went into self-shaming and self-loathing. I'm punishing myself for screwing up.

In meditation, I realized that Goddess doesn't work that way. Goddess loves us. And that provides a crucial insight.

If diets don't work, what does work?

Loving yourself works. You love yourself so much that when you choose what you eat and how you exercise. You feel that you're totally worth it. It could even become easy to lose the weight.

How so?

God and Goddess have given us the bounty of the earth. Good proteins, fruits and vegetables to fuel our bodies to grow and heal, and so much more. The God and Goddess want us to be all that we can be.

December of last year, my doctor warned me that I had to lose weight. My extra weight was aggravating my asthma. More than that, I did not want to succumb to diabetes like my mother.

However, I'd tried diets before and had failed miserably. What to do? Return to the Goddess. This time I'd approach the whole process differently. My journey would be about natural food (letting go, most of the time, of processed food and processed sugar). I'd incorporate ritual, keeping my sense of humor, protecting my personal energy and more.

I choose a different lifestyle—one that honors the God and Goddess and honors myself. I choose the Goddess Style Weight Loss way of living now. And it works.

I have lost 42 lbs. so far, and I feel so much better.

What do you do when you have good news? You tell someone! So, I wrote a book to help others.

It's time to choose. Love or myth—What do you choose?

Section Six:
Freedom to Be Me #3

The Dark Time

"What can I do now? I know that it's the dark half of the year, and Wiccans tend to shy away from spellwork at this time. What do you suggest?" my friend, Jessica, asked.

"It's a great time for inner work," I replied.

With Samhain passed (as of this writing), we can go into the vast landscape within. We can discover things about ourselves and how the world influences us.

Many of us, currently, do mirror work. However, this is advanced self-work and should not be tried without a High Priestess or another elder to guide you.

On the other hand, you can do the following exercises to address your inner world.

1. Meditation on Self-improvement

Meditation invokes great power. It can bring us up or bring us down.

Meditation serves as a doorway into the vast expanse of the mind. As you explore your own mind, you discover both the light half and the Shadow-Self half.

Now, in this dark part of the year, we find it to be a good time to work on the Shadow-Self.

Several years ago, I faced intense, personal self-esteem problems. (With a diligent practice and guidance of mentors, I have freed myself from much of my self-esteem difficulties.)

This following meditation really helped me when I needed it most.

May this meditation be helpful to you as you seek to shine light in the dark recesses of your mind. I offer this process, so you can enhance your self-esteem.

Self-Love Meditation
Close your eyes.
Breathe in and out deeply . . . Relax.
Keep breathing.
Breathe out the stress of the day.
Breathe in relaxation and peace.
(Pause)

You are still aware of the light that is in the room.
Now the light begins to fade.
As it fades you feel total comfort. You feel safe and secure in the darkness.
(Short Pause)

Now, a new form of light blossoms. It surrounds and wraps you in its loving energy. This light is the light of the Gods.

It is a light of love and compassion. Take it in.

As you take this light and understanding in, you can now see with the Gods' eyes.

You can now see yourself as they see you, pure, beautiful, whole. You are a masterpiece of Their creation. You were made with love, and you are a manifestation of Their love. You are love.

This understanding fills you.

(Pause)

With this new understanding you are now ready to return to the physical world.

You know that even though you may leave the light at this time it is never truly gone.

It's a gentle transition as the light begins to fade around you.

Slowly at first. It gets darker and darker.

As it fades you feel total comfort. You feel safe and secure in the darkness.

(Short Pause)

Then a familiar light returns, the light in the room where you started.

It gradually gets brighter and brighter.

You are back in the room. You have brought the calm and peace and happy feelings back with you.

Now, gently open your eyes.

I hope you find comfort with this meditation.

2. Make tinctures, balms, and potions from the herbs you collected earlier in the year.

This is a great indoor activity when the nights grow longer.

Infusion or Potion

What is an infusion or potion? They're the result of soaking herbs in hot water to bring out their properties. Human beings have healed themselves through herbs since prehistoric times. I suggest the book, *The New Healing Herbs: The Essential Guide to More Than 125 of Nature's Most Potent Herbal Remedies* by Michael Castleman.

Warning: only use herbs that you are certain to be food grade. Talk to your doctor before using any herb. Why? Herbs by themselves can cause harmful effects. For example, chamomile can cause uterine contractions which may lead to miscarriage, so pregnant women are advised to avoid chamomile!

Furthermore, herbs can mix with each other or with medications in harmful ways. You need accurate information before you ingest any herbs. Find credible professionals who have expertise in alternative medicine because many western medicine doctors do not have great knowledge in this area.

The simplest example of an infusion, brew or potion is tea. We drink teas, but not all potions or brews are meant to be ingested.

Second warning: Never make a potion with poisonous plants!

After you have done some research and consulted a doctor and have chosen a safe herb, you can make a tea. Heat water to almost a boil and add selected herbs into a ceramic container, like a cup.

Pour the water over herbs and place a cover to steep the brew. The cover keeps most of the steam in and this helps keep the essential oils in your potion. Then let the portion steep for about 5 to 10 minutes. Strain the mixture. We have been talking about tea; however, you can use brews for other uses. For example, you can use brews to cleanse spaces by asperging areas or by washing the floors and other surfaces with it. You may anoint things like sachets, talismans and amulets. Herbs may be used for a ritual bath. Once again, be sure the plants are safe for whatever use.

You can also use the sun to make potions. Take a clear jar and fill it with water and your herb mixture. Next place it in direct sunlight for six hours or so and then use.

You can use potions . . .
- for drinking in a tea (when appropriate)
- to wash your floors or wipe furniture.
- to augment your bath water for when you rest and soak.

Having a relaxing bath with a hot cup of tea on a cold winter night may be just what the Goddess ordered!

3. Concentrate on your bonds with friends and family.

The dark time serves well with opportunities for getting closer to friends, family, and the God and Goddess. Aim to strengthen your bonds with loved ones. Here is a recipe that will bring everyone together on a cold night.

Kay's Lamb Stew
2 packets Knorr's Leek Soup
2 tsp. Olive Oil
2 large cloves garlic
1 small bunch green onions
2 packets stewing lamb
3 Red Potatoes

Two packets of Knorr's Leek soup mix, made according to instructions, in a large pot on the stove so you can keep stirring it.

Next to the pot of soup, place into a deep-frying pan olive oil, on medium heat. Slice up two large cloves of garlic, one small bunch of green onions, and put them in the frying pan to cook for about 5-7 minutes, just to take the bite out of them.

Then (cut up meat beforehand in small rectangles) put in lamb meat a in frying pan to cook with garlic and onions. Brown the meat on all sides. Cook the meat through—just enough without being tough.

Put the lamb and onions into the soup, and have it on low to simmer. Cut up red potatoes into small rectangles and add them to the soup.

Then just keep the soup on simmer until the potatoes are done. This stew can be refrigerated and reheated, and it gets better with age.

* * *

In summary, Wiccans generally focus on spellwork during the light half of the year.

Now, in this dark half of the year, take advantage of opportunities to do inner work. As you've seen, we've covered powerful processes that offer you chances to grow and deepen in your Wiccan practice.

Section Six:
Freedom to Be Me #4

Wiccans and Hiding

Whether you're in the *broom closet* or not, many of us hide in some ways.

Hiding? From what?
- Hiding from ourselves –
- Hiding from what we want –
- Hiding from what hurts us –
- Hiding from hoping.

Can you relate to this?

In this dark half of the year (when this was written), many Wiccans find it a good time to do inner work.

"I am the Gracious Goddess, who gives the gift of joy unto the heart. Upon earth, I give the knowledge of the spirit eternal; and beyond death, I give peace, and freedom, and reunion with those who have gone before. Nor do I demand sacrifice, for behold I am

the Mother of All Living, and my love is poured out upon the earth." – *from* The Charge of the Goddess *by Doreen Valiente*

Did you notice this part? "Nor do I demand sacrifice." Isn't the fear of sacrifice part of why we hide? Have you noticed that we just don't like to give up what we have? We'll now look at different facets of our journey.

Hiding from Ourselves

You might think, why would I hide from myself?

Perhaps, you're hiding from a specific part of yourself. Sometimes, we can fear our own power. We may subconsciously want to believe that we are small and vulnerable. That seems easier. How? We can blame our problems on others and surrounding circumstances. And we do not have to do anything new.

Let's say that you let go of just playing small, what do you have? A responsibility.

Recently, my husband talked about his father's habitual statement: "You make me mad." My husband said, "My father just does not acknowledge that the recurring part of the equation is my father, and his often-terrible behavior connected to his own anger."

I thought about my husband's observation. It reminds me that *when we own a problem then we have the power*. As soon as we can stop hiding from our greatness, we will succeed in our endeavors in the mundane and on the magickal plane, too.

I have written about blocks and held workshops on removing them. You may want to reflect on your own journey. What might be a block for you in your own life?

One time, I was out walking, and these thoughts arose: *Mostly we are afraid of change, in ourselves and in the world around us. We are afraid of losing ourselves.*

We are also afraid of our darker self or Shadow Self, which can wreak havoc in our own life.

We, witches, delve deep into our subconscious and work with the Shadow Self to learn from it and embrace it.

The Shadow Self wants to stay powerful. In working with the Shadow Self, we can step into the driver's seat of our life.

How do we work with the Shadow Self? Many of us learn to work well with the Shadow Self through a guided meditation led by an elder.

Hiding from What We Want

Why would we hide from what we want? One word: Disappointment.

Have you been hit by the heart-searing pain of disappointment? Such pain certainly inspires many of us to give up on what we want.

To get what we want, many times, we must change, grow and stretch. Have you noticed that fear of change often rises up?

We hide our true power. Our power is great, and the fear of this power can be so strong that we hide our desires deep within ourselves.

Some of us may have "forgotten" what our heart wants. We may think we want change, but our subconscious mind wants to stay the same. Why? Our subconscious mind wants to stay safe. Change can be scary to our subconscious mind because change and trying new things tosses us out of our comfort zone. Then we fall into the land of potential pain and disappointment. No outcome is certain. What is the easiest path? Staying the same.

Hiding from What Hurts Us

Doesn't it make sense to hide from and get away from anything that causes us pain?

The tough truth is: Many times, pain helps us grow. Like growing pains. We need to grow and stretch. To learn our lessons in this incarnation, we must endure pain, sometimes.

Pain can serve as a teacher. As the toddler falls and skins her knee, she learns that something didn't work. In fact, she might learn to steady herself by holding onto the edge of the couch while she develops "her walking legs."

Wiccans can serve themselves by observing what causes pain and then coming up with a plan for rituals, prayers to the God and Goddess, chants and/or spells.

Step forward. Observe your pain. Do not let pain and the fear of pain to shut you down. Instead, reach out to the God and Goddess. They stand at the ready to help you.

Hiding from Hoping

Why would you hide from even hoping about something? Pain. Disappointment.

Hoping implies that we may lose what we truly desire. It gives us the unsettled feelings of possible loss.

I really have a hard time with this one. I don't even want to hope for the fear of losing what I desire.

This reminds me of a conversation I had with my husband.

"Do you think you might look forward to that trip?" he asked.

"No. I can't do it. What if it things don't come together?" I replied.

Later, I realized that I did not want to look forward to something because I had already anticipated the possibility of losing it.

I really need to work on this. I don't want to stall and get stuck in my life. I want to grow and move forward—spiritually and emotionally.

Can you relate to this?

Have you stopped hoping about things?

In summary, Wiccans, during this dark half of the year, can do some inner work.

Take a close look. Are you hiding from yourself, from what you want, and from what hurts you? Are you even hiding from hoping for anything to go well?

The Wiccan path is one of growth and even challenge. Inner peace begins with our taking an honest look at our pain and fear. Then, reach out to the God and Goddess. Conduct ritual and give voice to chants and prayers. Own your Wiccan path, and start to see truly magickal things manifest.

Section Six:
Freedom to Be Me #5

Wiccans Take Back Yule

"How do you feel about how the Western world has taken over Yule?" my friend, Susan, asked.

Sometimes, it does bother me to see that other people have taken over the Pagan traditions of the Yule Tree, Yule Log and more.

Then, I think about how we, Wiccans, can claim the Yule Season for our own hearts.

What Wiccans Emphasize About Yule

Let's look at the Yule Tree. Evergreens were seen as proof of everlasting life. Our ancestors saw that evergreen trees were the one source of life that continued to live and stay green throughout the year. Even in the deepest winter. They didn't die with the rest of the plants during the cold months. They were special.

Our ancestors celebrated this. They and we, modern

Pagans, consider the Yule Tree as sacred.

This is why our ancestors brought evergreens into their homes and decorated them with small gifts to the God and Goddess. Candles were placed on the bows of the trees (I do not recommend this due to the fire hazard). This is where Yule trees come from, and yes—Christians have adopted the Yule Tree as their "Christmas tree."

Still, we, Wiccans, can say to ourselves "Our Yule Tree!"

Wiccans Can Support Their Own Spirits Amid the Gift-giving Rush

Have you ever found yourself fretting about getting the "right" gifts for a bunch of people at this time of year? Many Wiccans feel the crush of not having the funds for much gift-giving.

For Pagans, exchanging gifts, at this time, is really about celebration. How?

Think about it. Why do you give gifts in the first place?

The first gifts were exchanged by our ancestors as a means of expressing joy for the Sun God's return.

Small gifts were hung on the branches of the Yule tree for the God and Goddess. Now, we give gifts between ourselves, too.

You can think "small and meaningful." Even giving a printed-out photo, placed in a frame (from a "dollar store") can be a good gift.

Wiccans Meet with Family and Focus on One's Chosen Family

An old comment is: "If you think you're enlightened, just attend a family reunion!"

Do you ever dread going to family reunions?

For Pagans, family reunions can be an extra burden. Many of us, for good reasons, must keep our Pagan path as our own secret.

Many of us fear being outed as a witch/Pagan. We hide our pentacle necklaces and other jewelry to conceal our true selves.

So, what is the solution?

Devote Time with Your Chosen Family

In a few days, I'll be attending a Yule party with my coven. What a relief! Being with likeminded people can really help with the loneliness/alienation/fear that comes with being around non-pagans. Especially this time of year!

Finding a place where you can share common ground with support can be a life saver. Really!

A significant number of people commit suicide at this time of year.

Instead, having a safe and loving place to share with others of like-mind can stop the loneliness/alienation/fear for a Pagan at this time.

In summary, Yule has always been our time. Smile to yourself and own it.

Section Six:
Freedom to Be Me #6

Oppression and the Pagan Path

Have you recently felt the pain of oppression in your life? We, witches, often see how other people's intolerance results in unfairness and worse toward Pagans.

"When any government, or any church for that matter, undertakes to say to its subjects, this you may not read, this you must not see, this you are forbidden to know, the end result is tyranny and oppression no matter how holy the motives."
– Robert A. Heinlein

With today's political and religious climate, oppression seems to be the norm. Racism, sexism, and religious prejudice apparently surround us.

Have you noticed any intolerance in our own community of witches?

Racism

One year, at a certain Pagan festival, I heard someone express racist comments in the hallway of the host hotel. This made me feel truly uncomfortable. I even felt anger rising up.

I can't even imagine being someone of color hearing such garbage! My own husband is a person of color, and we have had discussions about this topic.

What is going on here? We, witches, already know oppression. Why would any of us feel okay about expressing oppression within our own ranks?

As witches, we understand being oppressed. We remember the Burning Times. With the atrocities, the Church drove the Craft underground.

With our community still bleeding from such oppression, why would any of us be okay with oppressing another person? If I could talk to the person who expressed these racist comments I would say, "We are all children of the God and Goddess. They love us all, that's right, all! Remember, we are all part of the Gods, and, the Gods are part of us. There is no color in the God's and Goddess's eyes. We are one!"

Sexism

The overwhelming misogyny of the Burning Times is plain to see.

However, misogyny continues today. It's reported that women only earn $0.79 to every dollar that men earn. Why is this tolerated?

While I was reflecting on this, I realized something startling. In modern witchcraft, it appears that men are being marginalized. Many of us realize that "witch" is a term for both men and women. However, many people have the mistaken notion that a male witch is a "warlock" (wrong!). The word "warlock" is only used for people who break their oaths. And many male witches consider it a derogatory term, which it is. So, please don't call someone a warlock.

Think about it. It's October (at this writing), and you go into your favorite costume shop and look for a witch costume. Have you ever seen a male witch costume? I know I haven't.

Keep in mind that a male witch is just as important as female witches. Remember that the Goddess gets all Her power from the God. The God lays all His power at the feet of the Goddess because He knows She is just and fair.

Religious Prejudice

In the Burning Times, not only did our community face misogyny, anyone who thought differently than the Church was in jeopardy. This meant you could be charged for heresy if anyone heard your opinion and reported it.

Mostly women were affected, but men were also accused and killed (hanged/burned). Whole towns were wiped off the map during the Burning Times. Some have reported that leaders during the Burning Times used the accusations of heresy as a pretext to fulfill their political aims.

Even now, many of us stay in the broom closet. Why? Hatred toward witches persists to this day.

Many of us stay hidden because we don't want to be targeted by others' hatred.

"There are forms of oppression and domination which become invisible—the new normal." – Michel Foucault

This isn't just the witch thing either. It's also a race thing, and a sexism thing. It's oppression in its many forms.

As Witches, what do we do when oppression is expressed in our own community?

As witches, we need to reach out with understanding in our hearts.

"Peace cannot be kept by force; it can only be achieved by understanding." – Albert Einstein

"Compassion is more important than intellect in calling forth the love that the work of peace needs, and intuition can often be a far more powerful searchlight than cold reason." – Betty Williams

So, how do we reach understanding and compassion? With the God and Goddess, that's how.

Through meditation and ritual, the Gods can help us look within and discover the truth.

That truth is that we are all connected, both to the Gods and to each other. We are all equal in the light of the Gods. We may look different, have different abilities, and have different personalities; but we are all one.

Even though, in many ways, we cannot control our world leaders and the destructive cultural pressures around us, we can hold our own culture to a higher standard.

Lead with love and compassion towards others.

So, when you look into the eyes of a stranger, see yourself, see the God, and see the Goddess.

Section Six:
Freedom to Be Me #7

Magick and Science: A Wiccan Viewpoint

One of my readers asked this question: "It has been said that the scope of science is limited to the material world. How are people detecting the presence of the supernatural?"

I'll put this in as few of words that I can: Numerous examples exist of supernatural phenomenon occurring when a coven is doing ritual within a Circle.

However, this becomes somewhat difficult to discuss here. Why? Because of the phrase Wiccans say: "What happens in Circle stays in Circle."

Still, we can look at these three details:

a) Science measures energy. Magick is energy. Science could measure energetic phenomenon at some point.

Let's say a scientist was a coven member. If her fellow coven members would agree, it's possible that some scientific measurement instruments could be set up and run during Circle. We do not know if these particular instruments would detect* the movement of energy that occurs during a ritual.

* One notes various light detectors (or light meters). Light (or energy) operates as various forms: Light on the visible spectrum, infrared light, gamma rays and more. Different detectors can detect different things.

b) Science focuses on that which is replicable.
Science focuses on that which occurs and can be repeated (replicable) by others in various laboratories around the world. This sounds valuable as far as it goes. Is the energy raised in Circle going to be absolutely the same from coven to coven? No. It's not even the same from day to day in the same coven. So, already, we have a "structural" barrier here.

c) A Wiccan definition of "supernatural" is other than the conventional definition.
To me, casting Circle and doing a ritual is about the movement of natural energy. If a non-witch were to observe what happens in the Circle, that uninformed person would say something like: "I just saw something supernatural …"

However, I would disagree with this person's statement. The energy raised during a ritual is simply natural.

In summary, magick is energy. Some forms of energy can be detected with various scientific instruments.

Which instruments could "observe" magick created in Circle is likely not fully known.

The other complication is that most covens' rituals are private. (It's not like covens are running to colleges and saying, "Hey, measure this!")

Section Six:
Freedom to Be Me #8

The Wiccan Path of Freedom and Happiness

One of my friends, Glenn, said, "Something really bothers me about religion."

"What?" I asked.

"I just want to grab certain people by the collar and say, 'Stop terrorizing little kids!'"

"What are you talking about?"

"Hell!"

Wiccans have nothing to do with the notion that there is a Hell where people are said to be sent to burn for eternity (This is a proclamation of certain sects of Christianity.)

Imagine. In Wicca, we're free of the terror that one can sin and be forever condemned. Is torturing a person forever the plan of a loving God?

If you're not terrified by the thought that you'd burn, you may have more room for love and happiness in your life.

How so?

If you're not afraid of being punished and worried about being bad, you're probably going to be a happier person. You'd feel free and have a better relationship with the Gods.

You're not going to be afraid to talk to Them. You'll connect more often with the God and Goddess. You will take comfort in having the Gods in your life.

In a conversation with some friends, I listened to how some religions focus a lot on "rules."

"Why?"

One friend replied, "Because the people are scared. If they follow all the rules, the people think they'll be okay."

Wicca talks about how mistakes lead to consequences—but without all that "judgment for eternity" stuff.

Make a mistake. Make amends. Do better. Perhaps, you might continue to make amends in your next incarnation. NO eternal damnation.

Therefore, life (or this incarnation) is a classroom. The God and Goddess are supportive guides and teachers. Wicca is a loving and kind spiritual path.

Section Seven: Protect Yourself

"I need a protection spell," my friend, Amanda, said.

"What's going on in your life?" I asked.

"I'm going on a trip and I want to be safe while I travel," she said.

As we talked, it seemed that part of her situation was that she was beating herself up with her own thoughts.

"If that which thou seekest thou findest not within thee, thou wilt never find it without thee." – from The Charge of The Goddess *by Doreen Valiente (writing in the voice of the Goddess)*

Yes, there are times when having a protection spell *is* valuable. Still, I included the above quote from *The Charge of the Goddess* because we can find ourselves needing *to protect ourselves from our own disheartening thought patterns.* Goddess placed a certain form of peace *within you* as She created you. You just need practice to access *the peace within.* (In this book we mention meditation and specific rituals.)

Imagine the Goddess saying, **"I am always there for you. I always surround you. I am always within you."**

It's comforting to understand and feel this level of truth. And, we all get moments of doubt now and then. I could have asked, "Where were You, Goddess, when my 11-year-old brother held me underwater when I was 8-years-old? Terrifying me."

"I was there," Goddess would say, "—to make sure you did *not* drown in that swimming pool. I was there when you got the lesson that you need to learn to take care of yourself. I was there when you learned to carry on and move forward from the traumas you've endured. And I was there when you learned compassion for yourself and others who experienced abuse."

It's hard for me to write the above. I still hurt about the betrayal by my own brother. And then, I get the experience of feeling real empathy for anyone else going through such traumas.

If someone talks about attempting suicide, I feel empathy there, too. I attempted suicide after my parents' neglect and torture by my brother.

My point here is *Goddess sees the context of your whole life.* Related to the horrible moments when you didn't think you'd survive, Goddess can and does provide some comfort. You may not feel it right at that moment, but you can feel it later.

Even now, if you're seeking comfort and your current circle of friends does not provide that for you, know that *we* are here through this book.

We, Wiccans, have an advantage. We can do protection spells.

My purpose in bringing up the above details is to suggest, you could also include in your rituals something like:

"Goddess guide me. Goddess help me take every experience and use it to make me stronger, wiser and kinder. Thank you."

Section Seven:
Protect Yourself #1

Protect Yourself from Messing Up a Spell

"I'm afraid that I'll mess up my spells," my friend, Adriana, said.

"And?" I asked.

"And, I just don't do them often."

It's important to pay attention to a situation like this one. Wicca is a faith that is based on you taking action. Without doing spells or rituals, a witch simply does not grow and develop.

Here's the good news. You can place certain clauses into your magick spells and give yourself protection. Analogously, this reminds me of how lawyers use certain protective clauses in their documents.

What are clauses in magick?

Clauses are safeties you put on your spells—either to limit their effect or to keep things you don't want from manifesting. Clauses are worded like "an may it harm none" or "may this or better, with no harm to anyone."

Examples of protective clauses are found in my Money Manifesting Spell …

Money Manifesting Spell

As I light this candle so,
Make my money grow and grow,
Let it flow without rhyme or reason,
Each and every turn of season,
Filling up my pockets so wide,
Let me enjoy this happy ride,
Make me stronger than the ocean tides,
Manifesting my will to coincide,
With no malice, woe or hitches,
May there be no mess or jinxes,
With no need of fear of ruin,
Let it rain money, bless my journey.
An it harm none, so mote it be!

Now, we will take notice of the protective clauses.
You will notice the lines,
"With no malice, woe or hitches,
May there be no mess or jinxes,
With no need of fear of ruin,"

These lines are "clauses."

Why do we put protective clauses in our spell work?

We do so to protect ourselves and others. In the case of the clauses I shared above, we see "With no malice, woe or hitches." This keeps the spell from possibly backfiring and creating negative outcomes. The clause "May there be no mess or jinxes" serves to protect you from the spell manifesting in a way you do not want. And finally, there's the phrase "with no need of fear of ruin." Again, this is a clause that protects you and others from negative outcomes.

Where do the protective clauses go in my spells?

Protective clauses usually go at the end of a spell or chant. As in the example above, you can have multiple protective clauses.

In summary, it's good to have protective clauses. This process can help you quiet down fear and then you are likely to do more spellwork.

Section Seven:
Protect Yourself #2

Keep from Spiraling Down into a Low Mood—a Wiccan Solution

"Are you keeping up? Look what the administration is doing that's hurting Mother Earth!" my friend, Jeff, said. "I can't help it. With looking at the world and how I'm getting pushed around at work, my mood is lower than low. I've hit bottom."

Perhaps, you can relate to Jeff's concerns.

Have you awakened in the morning and felt unprepared to face the day and all its problems?

Maybe you're emotionally exhausted. Several of my Wiccan friends say, "Every time I see any broadcast news, I feel drained."

Are you feeling sad? Feeling sad is normal. A rough day or a rough patch of life can inspire sad feelings. We are not going to try to put a bow or happy face on feeling sad. The idea is: You can experience some sadness and then, at times, shift into another state of being.

Three Steps to Help You Climb Out of a Low Mood

1. Listen to Music – Chant – Sing

A big depression symptom that can knock me down is: Feeling that I have no energy. Sure, I know that if I could get myself to a coffee shop and sit with a friend, we'd have a good time talking. But the problem is that I feel that I have no energy. I'm having trouble getting out of bed.

What can we do?

Listen to music. In three clicks or less, you're listening to music. You could sing along.

Or you could do a bit of personal chanting or singing. You don't have to have great talent to do this. Just light a candle and express yourself. It helps.

The point is that music can lessen the burdens in your heart.

While listening to your preferred music, you could dance! Moving your body helps get the blood flowing and can shake out a bad mood.

Consider taking a walk while chanting, humming, or singing.

2. Meditate or Pray (Talk to the God and Goddess)

A version of an old phrase is: "When you meditate, you listen to Deity. When you pray, you talk to Deity."

Many of us Wiccans choose to connect with the Goddess. We pick a God or Goddess with whom we resonate.

Certain types of meditation can also help you beat a bad mood. Especially if you're subject to self-deprecating thoughts.

However, some people have hesitations about meditation.

They find it tough to sit in silence with their thoughts. Is that you?

My mother must have the T.V. on as soon as she gets up until bedtime. Why? Because she desperately does not want to have silence and hear her own thoughts. She is so unhappy that staying in her own thoughts troubles her greatly. She needs a pacifier of the T.V. to distract her from her thoughts.

A Solution If You're Afraid of Disturbing Thoughts During Meditation

Focus on a phrase that uplifts your heart. I use this phrase: "I am the Gods' Love; I am the Gods' Light." I use this phrase for a mantra.

3. Call Appropriate Friends—Get Outside

I've heard friends who deal with depression-symptoms say, "I'm a real actor. I pretend that I'm okay when I feel horrible." So, at times, it feels like we can't call people because we're afraid of "bringing them down, too."

Think about which friend is someone you don't have to pretend with. Talking with a good friend can reduce stress and, for females especially, can create oxytocin, known as the bonding hormone. This hormone helps you feel safe and bonded into your personal community.

Wiccans need our community to feel heard and to feel we have a common identity. Talking to people in our personal witch/pagan community can lift your mood.

Wiccans talking and listening to each other is vital because there are times when some of us may be targeted with disdain or even hate. Find someone who will support you.

I've noticed that it is good to realize that you can have different "levels" of friends. Some friends are stronger and closer. They can be good listeners to your difficulties. They can give you the support you need. And they are there when you need them.

Also, just getting out of your home into the sun may be just what you need. Especially during the dark half of the year. Get some fresh air, and it's better with a friend than without.

** Depression Symptoms Can Be an Alert to Other States of Being—Clinical Depression and S.A.D.

Those of us who deal with Seasonal Affective Disorder (SAD) find that this requires treatments like light therapy (phototherapy), psychotherapy and medications. Those who deal with SAD need to check with medical professionals.

The Mayo Clinic reports: "Seasonal Affective Disorder (SAD) is a type of depression that's related to changes in seasons—SAD begins and ends at about the same times every year. If you're like most people with SAD, your symptoms start in the fall and continue into the winter months, sapping your energy and making you feel moody. Less often, SAD causes depression in the spring or early summer."

There are other forms of depression, too. In these cases, you need to consult medical professionals for help.

About Clinical Depression

Every day, I deal with the symptoms of clinical depression. The Mayo Clinic reports:

"Depression is a mood disorder that causes a persistent feeling of sadness and loss of interest. Also called major depressive disorder or clinical depression, it affects how you feel, think and behave and can lead to a variety of emotional and physical problems. You may have trouble doing normal day-to-day activities, and sometimes you may feel as if life isn't worth living."

A "Combination Approach" to Dealing with Symptoms of Clinical Depression

I deal with all of the above problems. I have been fighting for decades to keep myself alive and well.

I've seen it in the eyes of people who are free of symptoms. It's as if they're saying, "Oh, you're feeling sad. Just buck up and carry on!" These people are uniformed about the reality of clinical depression. I can describe it as trying to climb a mountain and you only have one pint of blood in your body. You have no energy, no resources ... and at times, no hope. Oh—and don't forget the associated anxiety!

I have used a Combination Approach to survive and thrive. I was lucky that I was diagnosed early in my life. An effective combination of medication and doctor/ psychiatrist /therapy and the God and Goddess has helped significantly in my life.

With the Gods on my side helping me, I'm leading a better life.

* * *

In summary, I've shared three methods, so you can shift from a low mood. The goal is not to attempt to avoid all low moods. That's not possible. The idea is to, perhaps, shift sooner out of a low mood.

Additionally, I suggest that you consider using a calendar

to schedule your meditation (perhaps, make it daily?). Also, call appropriate friends and create reoccurring times to get together. Maybe, you'll set up a weekly girls/bros night out.

As Wiccans we do well to schedule time for meditation, prayer and ritual to connect with the God and Goddess. Remember, They want to support you. The God and Goddess are there waiting to share Their wisdom and comfort with you.

Section Seven:
Protect Yourself #3

Protect Yourself from Big Samhain Mistakes—and Enjoy the Best of this Sabbat

"I don't think I'll ever do that supper ritual again!" my friend, Amanda said.

"What happened?" I asked.

"We invited the spirits of our dead friends and family members to the ritual supper, and they did *not* leave! Over the next days, I felt really depressed. I later learned that my friend, Alex, was hovering near me. I was being haunted," Amanda said.

This is a real problem if one fails to do the appropriate precautions for a specific Samhain dinner, titled a "Dumb Supper." The word dumb refers to "unable to speak."

We (my coven) will soon hold our annual Dumb Supper. This is a ritual meal eaten without talking or even making a peep.

You invite your deceased loved ones by setting a place for them at the table. It is so nice to visit with departed friends and family members. Sometimes, you can hear them, and sometimes they show signs that they are present. For example, one of my coven mates told me she saw a sign swing back and forth waving "Hi." It really moved her heart.

Be sure to "kick out" departed friends and family members after the celebration is done. You do not want them hanging around. After you have shared your time with them, make sure they go back to the Land of the Dead where they belong.

I have heard of situations when a departed family member desperately tried to express his sorrow and attempts to apologize. Unfortunately, the living family member felt depressed or even scared.

Here is an example of language to send the spirits away: "Thank you for participating during our supper. We now send our departed family members and departed friends back to the Summerlands. We now Close the Veil. So Mote It Be."

Ever wonder what you should and shouldn't do during Samhain? Here are some quick tips for this Sabbat. This is just a partial list.

The Do's:
1. Honor your departed friends and family

Samhain is my favorite Sabbat. We honor those who have crossed the Veil with offerings and recalling memories of them when they were alive.

When you make offerings and bring up memories of your loved ones who have crossed over to the Summerlands, you bring them alive again in your own heart and others' hearts.

Some things you can do are simple. You could fix their favorite meal or drink. Give them a toast with that drink with good energy and love.

2. The most important thing ... Have fun!

This is a joyful time where we get to get to visit with our departed loved ones. Do you think that they want you to be sad? No. Our departed loved ones want us to be happy.

When you see or hear your departed loved ones, allow a smile to rise to your face. And, it's also okay to have tears of joy when being reunited with departed loved ones.

The Don'ts:
1. Don't get upset with the Mundanes

Don't fret over the general society's way of celebrating Samhain. Yes, they have taken and distorted some things from us, Pagans. Be kind. They don't know any better. Instead, enjoy the festivities. You don't have to be a downer to the Mundanes. Hand out candy. And have some fun.

2. Don't do your ritual on the October 31st

There will be too many distractions with answering the door and handing out goodies to the little ones in the evening. This is the reason why many witches celebrate on either the weekend before or after October 31st.

3. Don't forget the Ancestor Altar

Having an Ancestor Altar is really fun, and it's a must for Samhain. Decorate your altar with pictures of passed loved ones and include your departed pets! Witches love their animals. And yes, they go to the Summerlands, too.

Just imagine ... those of us who have had a lot of pets

over the years, we're going to get mobbed with love when our numerous pets greet us in the Summerlands!

These are just some of the do's and the don'ts.

Consider asking others about their experiences. We can learn from each other.

Let's make each Samhain one to remember fondly.

Section Seven:
Protect Yourself #4

Don't Get Caught Up in Someone Else's Labeling of People

One of my readers asked this question: "Are Christian Pagans and Wiccans a new attempt by Christians to mock and make actual Wiccans and Pagans submit to their beliefs?"

As I reflected on this question, these areas come up in my thoughts.

1. "Christian Wiccan" as a term

This term does NOT work for me because the ideas of Christianity and Wicca disagree about the Divine.

In the *Christian Bible,* Jesus is quoted as saying "I am the way and the truth and the life. No one comes to the Father except through me (John 14:6)." That sounds like an exclusionary idea.

Wicca is about having a relationship with the old Gods

and Goddesses. So, we have monotheism (Christianity) disagreeing with polytheism (Wicca).

2. The idea of some Christian individuals trying to appropriate a Pagan focus—like Yule Trees "became Christmas trees."

About your comment about "a new attempt by Christians to mock and make actual Wiccans and Pagans submit to their beliefs": several scholars mention how Christians "appropriated" Pagan days into their own calendar (including December 25th and Easter—which Wiccans know as Ostara ... and more).

In this book, I've included a section on "Wiccans Take Back Yule."

My point of view is that it is up to Wiccans to keep their own spiritual path clear and sacred.

3. The Freedom of an individual to combine elements into her own spiritual path

Let's say an individual, Jill, says that she believes in "Jesus, the Goddess and ritual and magick." Perhaps, she can call herself "eclectic."

4. Using language as a path for understanding

There are times, as I write my books, when I go back to definitions of words. In another section of this book, I noted *enthusiasm* with a Latin origin including "theos" which means God. The definition includes "inspired by God"—and *inspire* means "breathe life into."

A conversation works better when the participants can come to a working definition of key words.

This brings me back to how I dislike the term "Christian Wiccan." By definition, the words do *not* go together.

Section Seven:
Protect Yourself #5

Work with Spirit Guides

Spirit Guides can participate in your protection. Years ago, I went into a meditation for the express purpose of meeting my Spirit Guide. That's when my Spirit Guide Linda appeared.

I've written on my blog about how a significant number of us seek to protect ourselves by gaining and developing a big body as a shield.

Rita, a friend, said, "It was like I was saying, 'See! I'm no longer a tiny girl that you can abuse!'"

Think about it. With a big body, the scared, vulnerable you on the inside might feel safe.

As I wrote in *Goddess Style Weight Loss* (my book and online course), I observe the idea that dropping weight can be like dropping our shield. Why would we do that when the world proved to us that there are those who have hurt us—and others who might hurt us still?

In place of the big body, what or who will protect us?

The good news is: The God, Goddess and Spirit Guides are with you always—24/7.

"But I don't feel Their presence!" Rita said.

This is understandable. Why? Because we're often under the assault of "The Monkey Mind." That's the part of our thinking that "chatters" with distractions and fears.

That's the point. We don't feel the presence of God, Goddess and Spirit Guides because we're distracted by The Monkey Mind. (For example, I just felt the urge to check email on my smartphone.)

The answer is to step away from the chattering. For example, my husband meditates for three minutes every day. Just today, he said, "I didn't feel peace until about 2 minutes and 50 seconds into my meditation. But I did reach the peaceful experience."

The next step is to identify when, where and how you can feel the presence of God, Goddess and Spirit Guides. We see Their presence every day. From the grass between our toes to the mountains that are Their cathedrals.

We can Cast a Circle and do a ritual which takes us out of our daily, Monkey Mind, routine.

But what about inside of us?

We are even distracted by feelings in our bodies.

There is a solution: Eat in healthy ways.

Eating healthy helps us run our bodies with the fuel they were meant to have. Goddess, through human history, has provided the bounty that sustains us. It's only in modern times, when people have poisoned ourselves with processed, so-called food.

Realize that with healthy eating choices, our bodies will run better and with that comes a tighter bond in the ever-loving arms of the Gods.

In this way we will be closer to Them, and we have a better chance of physically feeling Them within ourselves. It's easier to connect with God and Goddess during a meditation if your body is not suffering from feeling bloated.

To bring this full circle, we're been talking about who guards you.

You guard yourself by making healthy choices.

Even better, when you do things to reduce the distractions of the Monkey Mind, you open the door to the presence of God, Goddess and Spirit Guides.

Just like being in Circle, you can have a spiritual experience when you go Goddess Style: Eating from the earth and honoring the beings you consume.

The truth is: Having a big body can hold you back from experiences you really want. (I must say at 42 pounds lighter, it is easier for me to fit into a seat on a jet plane!)

Having a big body apparently was something I needed at one time.

Now, I'm focused on who really guards me—myself, God and Goddess.

Would you like to make the transition to feeling the presence of God, Goddess and Spirit Guides?

Bonus Material

Bonus Material #1

Question: Wicca and many other real-world magic cultures are mostly or even exclusively female. Why? Were men believed to be able to perform magic, and if not, why not? Was it just cultural, or are there reasons tied to the magic itself?

Answer: I will address the Wicca portion of your question. Wicca is *not* mostly or even exclusively women.

In Wicca, a witch is either male or female.

Additionally, women are known to use and listen to their intuition more than many male individuals. A number of observers suggest that women, as connected with their intuition, are closer to the unseen world of spirits, Gods and Goddesses.

Eastern spiritual practices refer to yin and yang—yin as receptive and yang as the active, male principle. Every human being has both yin and yang as part of their makeup.

Men can access their intuition and their feminine energies.

Wicca does celebrate feminine strength and power. And, many women are drawn today to the Pagan path because of the empowerment of women.

Bonus Material #2

Chant to the Sun God

With Litha just passed (as I wrote this), we start our journey back to the dark part of the year. The God now begins to wane in power at Lughnasadh, when we celebrate the first of the harvest for this year.

How can we support the God through the waning season? Here is a simple candle ritual to help the God persist in His activities.

Light a gold or yellow candle and say the chant below.

Chant to the Sun God

Lord of the Sun, Lord of plenty.
We give you strength, we'll be your sentry.
Guarding your strength, till the last harvest's in.
Let the Sun God be strong!

Blessings to you in this time of fruitfulness.

Bonus Material #3

Question: Why is the TV/Movie viewing public so obsessed with supernatural abilities when in reality very few who can actually perform such feats?
Answer: It likely arises from how vulnerable human

beings are to physical damage.

A child takes a fall off playground equipment and breaks her arm. Sure, she'd like to invulnerable like *Supergirl*.

Or a friend gets whiplash in a car accident. Wouldn't it be great to have the healing powers of *ET* (1982 feature film)?

Regarding Wicca, practitioners do magick. Sometimes, the resulting healing appears miraculous or supernatural. However, my own mentors emphasized that the magick process is not supernatural. Instead, it is harnessing natural energies to create change. "Supernatural" implies "above the laws of nature." Wiccan do not engage in such a process.

In TV/movies, seeing supernatural feats is dramatic—and it's fun to watch.

TV/movies are about giving rise to feelings. Having a hero come in and save us can feel good—especially with all the calamities we're exposed via broadcast news.

Wicca is a natural process. Healing may take some days. It's not dramatic like TV/Movies. Wicca is also a hard-earned skillset.

Bonus Material #4

Question: "Do I need to have Gods to be a traditional witch?"

Answer: My first reflex was to reply, "Yes!"

Then I paused and thought about it. What might this person be thinking that leads to this question?

Perhaps, he or she thinks that a witch is simply someone who wields natural energy to create change. (That would be a sorceress.)

Maybe this person thinks that witches merely do spells to heal people and attract prosperity. (Still a sorceress.)

On the other hand, traditional witchcraft is about honoring the Old Gods. So, by definition, the answer is: "Yes. You need to honor the Old Gods to be a traditional witch."

Then, we look at what tradition attracts you. The Gardnerian tradition has its own particular pantheon of Gods. By the way, I won't be writing here about which Gods these are. Why? This knowledge is Oath Bound. One needs to be an initiated member in good standing with a Gardnerian coven to eventually learn of these Gods.

Still, one could look into various pantheons.

Here are a couple of examples:
(There are *many* more Gods in the below-referenced pantheons. The below list is just to give you a "taste.")

Norse Pantheon
Odin – father of all the Gods
Thor – son of Odin God of thunder
Freya – Goddess of love and beauty
Freyr – God of fertility

Greek Pantheon
Hera – Goddess of marriage and intrigue
Hercules – God of strength and adventure
Hermes – God of travel and commerce
Hestia – Goddess of home and family

Celtic Pantheon
The Daghdha – God of weather and crops
Arawn – God of life and death
Belenus – God of sun, light, and warmth
Brigantia – Goddess of rivers and livestock

Egyptian Pantheon
Ra-Horakhty – God of the sun, ruler of the gods
Anubis – God of judgment and death
Bastet – Goddess of cats and vengeance
Hathor – Goddess of love, music, and motherhood

In summary, the traditional witch does multiple things: She or he honors the Old Gods and works with magick to create change.

Your *Break Free with Goddess* Path Continues

As we complete this journey with this book, I celebrate your efforts and spiritual growth.

Please continue your path with me by viewing my articles at my blog at GoddessHasYourBack.com

Let's look at how far we have come. We have explored:
1. Freedom from Worry
2. Freedom to Express Yourself
3. Freedom to Be Healthy
4. Freedom for Abundance
5. Freedom to Be Creative
6. Freedom to Be Me
7. Protect Yourself

From this point forward, consider learning more about rituals, chants, tips, and ways to customize your rituals just for you ... and even more material when you sign up for my exclusive enewsletters. Just go to GoddessHasYourBack.com and click on the link (on the right side of the webpage).

Consider my previous seven books. Thank you.

Blessed Be,
Moonwater SilverClaw

Get Real Support. Take the 5-Week Online Course:

ABOUT THE AUTHOR

Moonwater SilverClaw is a Wiccan High Priestess and member of the Covenant of the Goddess and the New Wiccan Church. She has trained people new to Wicca. Her personal story reveals how Wicca saved her life and helped her strengthen herself to secure her release from an abusive marriage.

Moonwater has been practicing Wicca since 1990, first as a solitary and then in a coven.

Moonwater posts at her blog,

GoddessHasYourBack.com

[with visitors from 191 countries]

She felt called to write the blog and write 8 books even though she is dyslexic. She works with a team of editors. At Quora.com, Moonwater has been listed as "Most Viewed Writer" in the category "Witchcraft (Historical)." Quora.com visitors have viewed her answers over 73,000 times.

Moonwater has addressed college students in Comparative Religion classes for over ten years. She leads workshops. She lives with her cat Magick and her sweetheart of many years; he is one of her editors. She enjoys knitting and photography.

Her work is endorsed by Wiccan notables including Patrick McCollum (receiver of the Mahatma Gandhi Award for the Advancement of Religious Pluralism).

Moonwater SilverClaw can be contacted at:
AskAWitchNow@gmail.com
Or at her blog:
GoddessHasYourBack.com

Special Offer Just for Readers of this Book:
Contact Moonwater SilverClaw at askawitchnow@gmail.com for special discounts on books, consulting, workshops and presentations. Just mention your experience with this book.

Excerpt from

Goddess Has Your Back

by Moonwater SilverClaw

CHAPTER 1:
GODDESS HAS YOUR BACK

Would you like your Wiccan path to lift up your self-esteem?

Would you simply like to feel better?

This book helps you actually feel your connection with

the Goddess on a daily basis—even moment to moment.

As I mentioned in my first two books, *The Hidden Children of the Goddess* and *Beyond the Law of Attraction to Real Magick*, Wicca saved my life and empowered me to leave an abusive marriage.

As a High Priestess, I have supported friends, family, and colleagues in times of need. My blog GoddessHasYourBack.com gives me a weekly opportunity to support website visitors from 191 countries.

This book gives *us* the space and time to really explore magickal practices, rituals, meditations and experiences that you'll find comforting and uplifting.

My journey upon this path began with meeting the Gods. The Gods showed me the true path to self-love and acceptance. Where I saw nothingness and unworthiness, they showed me abundance and a unique specialness that I had.

Now I will let you in on a secret. *You have your own unique specialness that no one else has.* It is yours, and yours alone. This new path is yours to discover and walk. Just like my own path, your path is a beautiful discovery simply waiting for you. Prepare to step forward on this new, wondrous, and beautiful path.

Let's take the next step.

Secret of How to Do Magick

When I first started doing magick it was really hit or miss, most often *mess*. My spell work was just not as effective as I wanted it to be. What was I doing wrong?

If you have wondered the same thing, you have probably done similar mistakes. For example, I'd do a money spell, but I'd just get new problems!

The real problem was, like many people, I just wanted a

big payday. What I didn't know was that this is really the wrong way to approach a lack of money.

Many, if not most, spells written today are focused on the external opportunities or even requesting gifts from the Gods. Focusing on just the external can create new problems.

What if I could tell you a **Secret of how to do magick**—in a way where you avoid ethics issues about money?

I have mentored a number of people about this *Secret*. Now I will share with you this Secret.

A phrase from the poem by Doreen Valiente entitled *The Charge of the Goddess* tells us how to do magick well. But many of us, like my younger self, just don't see it. The line I'm talking about is: "...if that which thou seekest thou findest not within thee, thou wilt never find it without thee."

This line invites us to look within as we approach our magickal work.

Instead of focusing on how to get money from outside sources, focus within. How? Instead of asking for a handout from the universe, ask, **"How I can create more energy in myself to obtain my desire? How can I make myself open to more prosperity?"**

Let's get more specific. ...

END OF EXCERPT from the book *Goddess Has Your Back* Available from top online retailers.

* * * * * *

Read an excerpt from **Beyond the Law of Attraction to Real Magick**—on the next page.

Excerpt from

Beyond the Law of Attraction to Real Magick
How You Can Remove Blocks to Prosperity, Happiness and Inner Peace

by Moonwater SilverClaw

Self-perspective: Overcome the Blockage of Not Feeling Worthy

Do you feel worthy of the best that life has to offer? Maybe on the conscious level you say, "Sure. Bring it on. The new house, new car, and a real, loving relationship."

But have you ever sabotaged your chances of getting exactly what you wanted?

Self-sabotage can occur because of feeling not worthy on a subconscious level.

If it's subconscious, how can we deal with this?

Good question.

Soon I will share with you a Self-Love Meditation.

But first let's talk about magick. The whole premise of this book is that there is a way to go about the Law of Attraction with more power.

To put it simply, the Law of Attraction is a form of magick, but people who read an introductory book on the Law of Attraction are often denied enough information to truly make the Law of Attraction work in their own lives.

So, to really make a positive difference in your life, we need to talk about real magick. I spell magick with a "k" to distinguish it from stage magic you see on television.

Magick is a natural power, *not* a supernatural one. Who uses magick? In my spiritual path, Wicca, one is trained to use magick in appropriate ways.

When Wiccans do magick, they channel *natural* energies and create change with them.

Well, if Wicca isn't really supernatural then why practice Wicca at all?

To put it simply, *you want something*. That's probably why you were interested in the Law of Attraction in the first place. Now in the context of learning real magick, you'll be able to fully use the Law of Attraction. And that's good news!

Everyone is different and has their own answer to the question of why practice Wicca. I like to think of religion as a bottle of wine. Let's say you have three different people who all taste the same bottle of wine. The first person points out that the flavor has accents of oak. The second praises the hints of apple in it, and the third enjoys the floral notes. They are all right. The wine contains all the flavors they described. But each person detected something different. Religion is like that. Deity can't be entirely known. So, the truth of it is scattered into many faiths.

In Wicca, we honor the God and the Goddess. If that's new to you, you can substitute the label of Higher Power or God or Deity.

The Gods and Goddesses have helped me, and They can help you, too. The first thing they taught me was self-love.

Before we go further, let's make a distinction between self-love and self-conceit (or being stuck in one's ego).

Self-love is about kindness and support. So, it's a good thing. It is NOT about your ego or puffing yourself up.

Let me show you how the Gods changed my perspective on myself for the better.

One of the best exercises I learned is meditation. Through reflective meditation, the Gods helped me understand how skewed my perception of myself really was. This was a key turning point for me.

One thing you always hear about are affirmations, but for many of us these just don't work.

First, let's cover what an affirmation is. It's a personal, positive statement. It can be as simple as "I feel terrific" or "I make a lot of money."

For many, the above statements don't work. Why?

A number of people have said, "It just sounds like I'm lying to myself."

Like myself, many people's inner self-beliefs interfere with these positive statements. For an example, if I used the affirmation "I am thin," my brain would object with "No, I'm not. Look in the mirror." It's not true. No matter how hard you try to pound that new idea into your brain, your brain pounds just as hard back.

So how did the Gods help me deal with this problem? They inspired me to create a Self-Love Meditation.

So instead of the uphill battle of an affirmation, we'll use the Self-Love Meditation to work with the situation.

END OF EXCERPT from *Beyond the Law of Attraction to Real Magick*

Purchase your copy of the above books (paperback or eBook) at top online retailers.

See **Free Chapters** (at a top online retailer) of *Moonwater SilverClaw's 8 books*—including *Be a Wiccan Badass*.

www.ingramcontent.com/pod-product-compliance
Lightning Source LLC
Chambersburg PA
CBHW060534100426
42743CB00009B/1530